FREE GIFT

* * * * * * *

Thank you so much for your support. I am extending a free 15-minute purpose planning session to everyone who has purchased this book.

Discovering your purpose will change your life and give you a launching pad for your destiny. Whether you are fifteen or forty-five, it's never too late to pursue your dreams.

If you want to brainstorm with me about moving your life forward, visit my website at adriennemayfield.com, and book a free 15-minute consultation using the code "BURNING BUSH."

BURNING BUSH
—— BOOKS ——

Donnette,

The grace for multiplication is your portion. Everything your hand touched will grow and expand. Take advantage of this unique opportunity and dream bigger. An encounter with God transforms us — you're due for a new refreshing — Connect!

CONNECTING WITH THE BURNING BUSH

Adrienne Mayfield, Esq.

BURNING BUSH
BOOKS

BURNING BUSH
——BOOKS——

Connecting with the Burning Bush
by Adrienne Mayfield

Published by Burning Bush Books

Copyright © 2017 by Adrienne Mayfield

First edition December 2017

For information about bulk purchases, please contact Adrienne Mayfield at amayfield2147@gmail.com.

Manufactured in the United States of America

ISBN: 978-0-9997694-0-9

ISBN: 978-0-9997694-1-6 (E-BOOK)

All Scripture quotations, unless otherwise noted, taken from the Holy Bible, New King James Version.

Cover Design: Adrienne Mayfield and Paula Palmer-Green

Cover Image: Desy Suryani

Visit the author's website at adriennemayfield.com

This book is dedicated to those who have longed for an encounter with the God of their destiny

TABLE OF CONTENTS

ACKNOWLEDGEMENTS

I want to thank Abba for his unconditional love for me. You have been my calm in the storm, my shelter and strength, and my steady foundation. Without you, I never would have had the desire or courage to write this book. Words cannot express all you have meant to my life. Even when I wanted to quit, you never gave up on me. Your relentless pursuit of me has stolen my heart. My answer to you is "Yes, unequivocally, Yes!" I love you.

I would like to thank my grandparents and parents who have all joined the great cloud of witnesses who are interceding on my behalf in heaven. You left a tremendous legacy of faith and dependence on God. You were all people of great perseverance and prayer. Your legacy motivates me to run my race with grace.

To Dr. Charles F. Stanley of First Baptist Atlanta, Dunwoody. As a young girl, I sat at my grandparent's house and watched you preach the Word of God with fervor and passion. As a young woman, I sat as a member of FBA for six years. It was immediately after my home church had a very contentious split. I desperately needed Truth so that I would not give up on church altogether. Each week, you taught a bold and convicting lesson from the Word of God that challenged me to grow and expand my faith. That foundation is the very thing I stand on today. "We stand strongest and tallest on our knees." Thank you for challenging me to be like Jesus.

To Bishop James L. Dutton, Jr., Augusta. In 2000, I began attending your church. As someone who had been raised in a Baptist church, many of the things you preached about were foreign to me. Still, you gave me the opportunity to sing on the praise team and taught me about Holy Spirit. You also laid hands on me so that I could receive the infilling of Holy Spirit and speak in tongues. I still remember many of the sermons you preached. They strengthened my faith and deepened my relationship with the supernatural. Thank you.

To Dr. Matthew L. Stevenson III of All Nations Worship Assembly, Chicago: Your revelatory teachings and passion for holiness and worship have catapulted me deeper into the realm of the Spirit. Since World Changers 2016, my life has never been the same.

To Pastor Mark Smith of Abundant Life Church, Cumming: You saw greatness in me. The first time I visited your church, I asked you for prayer. You took me to a circle of women who laid hands on me and prayed the darkness away. You also believed in the gift of God in me and you encouraged me to use it. In one of the darkest moments of my existence, you were one of my biggest cheerleaders. Your confidence in my gift and destiny ushered me into my next season. Thank you.

To my brother, Kevin: You provided me with a safe place to heal and be replenished. You pushed me when I thought I had nothing left. You have been my biggest supporter. You have also taught me how to disciple someone by being consistently stubborn. ☺ You are the world's best big brother. Thank you.

To Pastor Frankie and Minister Oshea Vega: You have cultivated a people who love to worship God. At the Awakening and Reformation Center (ARC), I always felt the freedom to enter the throne room of God with reckless abandon. Thank you.

To Apostle Buddy and Prophet Mary Crum of the Life Center, Dunwoody: Your commitment to provide training for the body of Christ has been invaluable. At your church, I received prophetic ministry, was trained in the prophetic, received healing and deliverance, prophetic presbytery, and obtained a constant reminder that I am working to leave a legacy that transcends my days on Earth. Thank you.

To Prophet Catherine Sykes: Your teaching and training equipped me to walk in the gifts of the spirit. You imparted your gift of healing and gave me the confidence to embrace the call on my life. Your legacy of impartation and training are a gift to the Body of Christ. Thank you.

To Philip Watson: I am eternally grateful that you gave God a "yes" when he asked you to do Soak Scopes. Because of your obedience, I came to know God in a greater depth than I ever thought possible. You helped me see God even when I was in a very dark place. When you prophesied to me, I'm sure you were just being obedient, but God used you to shift my season and give me the title for this book. You are a tremendous blessing to the body of Christ. Thank you.

To Medgar: You are an amazing wordsmith. Your command of the English language is flawless. You are a master. I look forward to seeing your story in print. Thank you for giving me enough "soft" critique to push me to share the whole story. You also have the unique ability to slice through an entire sentence without destroying the passion for writing. Your editing and review were priceless. Thank you.

The Angel of the Lord appeared to him in a blazing flame of fire from the midst of a bush; and he looked, and behold, the bush was on fire, yet it was not consumed. So Moses said, "I must turn away and see this great sight—why the bush is not burned up." When the Lord saw that he turned away to look, God called to him from the midst of the bush and said, "Moses, Moses!" And he said, "Here I am."

FOREWORD

Have you ever wondered why you were born? The quest for purpose and destiny is common to the human experience. There is likely no person who has not at some point wondered what they should do with their life, whether they are on the right track, or if "this" is really all there is. Society gives us a picture of what the perfect life should look like—a great job, marriage, children, cars, money, and a huge house. We buy into the myth and join the rat race to success that is actually just a never-ending hamster wheel. In reality, there will always be someone with more. Someone will always have a bigger house, bigger car, prettier wife, more athletic husband—you fill in the blank! Trying to discover our value and worth from these things will always leave us feeling empty. Worse still, our quest to fill the void and gain validation can lead us through destructive cycles of pain and heartbreak.

Most often we are stagnated by our impatience. We live in a microwave society that tells us everything should happen now. We don't like to wait for anything—food, love, our dry cleaning, or our destiny. When "life" happens, and things aren't shaping up to what we always envisioned, we can become discouraged and want to give up.

Though we often mistake disappointment and frustration as the denial of our dreams, it is usually not the case. Most times, what we perceive as delay is simply God orchestrating the events that lead us to an optimal outcome. He always has our best in mind. I've often heard it said that "God is in the details." Nothing happens by accident. God is always at work behind the scenes. Every choice and every decision is intricately woven together by Him. He is omniscient; even our missteps and detours are woven into His perfect plan.

Like many of you, I discovered my purpose through a series of unfortunate events. I come from a family of educators. Therefore, I always thought that God's purpose for my life was simply to educate children. Both of my aunts were teachers, my sister is an elementary principal, and five out of six of my first cousins are teachers as well. As a young child I found myself excited about learning. I watched enviously as my older siblings read books; when they refused to read to me at will, I retorted, "You just wait! One day I will be able to read for myself, and I'll read all the books I can!"

Early in my childhood I also developed an affinity for teaching. I tried to teach everyone around me: my siblings, my friends, my parents, even the pets. One of the first Christmas presents I asked for was a chalkboard so I could practice. When none of my friends or cousins would agree to be students, I'd meticulously use my dolls instead.

As I journeyed through school, I never wavered in my desire to become a teacher. I graduated from high school and left for college. I taught high school English and became an assistant principal. I began pursuing what I thought was God's plan for my life. For eleven years I chased the dream of being a career educator. I obtained two degrees and started climbing the ladder, but I knew deep inside there was something more for me. Though I enjoyed impacting the lives of young people, I started to feel like something was missing.

I knew I was making an impact. Many of my students went to college, but those accomplishments paled in comparison to the overwhelming needs I saw. Those small successes were simply like a rock thrown into a pond. I never wanted to be like that rock. I always wanted to do something spectacular. I wanted to change the world. I wanted to make a difference. I wanted my legacy to the world to function like a tidal wave--something that would be far-reaching and remembered for years to come.

My unfulfilled desires led me to abandon teaching to enter law school at the age of 37. It was no easy feat as I found myself competing with youngsters who could have easily been my former students. I had not been a student for over 14 years; many of my classmates had just completed their undergraduate degrees. Still, I felt the nudge of God pushing me to embark on this quest, so I acquiesced.

To the outside world, I was at the top of my game. The truth was--I wasn't! I had suffered a series of tremendous setbacks that shook me to my core. Everything in the natural world taught me that I should be complete. I had the education, the degree and credentialing that placed me in the top tier of society. I was successful by societal standards, but I was also horribly broken. Deep inside, my soul cried out for something greater.

How could I discover what the "something greater" was? How could I ascertain what the source of this deep yearning in my soul was about? How could I find the healing I so desperately needed? Apparently I needed an entire course correction. That course correction came in the form of a series of intense encounters with God. Through them, I gained new perspective and begin to make sense of the last ten years of my life. I am on a different path now, but none of that would have been possible had I not been accosted by the God of my destiny. My purpose and power did not begin to unfold until I "Connected with the Burning Bush."

INTRODUCTION

The story of Moses is one of the most well-known narratives in history. Most people have seen Charlton Heston lift his rod, part the Red Sea, and lead the children of Israel across on dry land in the television version of the Ten Commandments. What Christian hasn't heard or read about the plagues of Egypt, Pharaoh's stern refusal, or the rebellious children reveling around the golden calf they made? Few people, religious or otherwise, are unfamiliar with these stories.

It is said that familiarity breeds contempt and that often becomes the case with stories and people that are common to us. Sometimes we miss the wisdom and deeper meaning because we believe we are experts on the subject. Most people would probably claim to know something about Moses and his role in delivering the children of Israel. What many people miss, however, is the parallel between their lives and the divine encounter God seeks to have with them.

Moses is a very unique character in the Bible. He was born in a very difficult time. In fact, his very birth had to be concealed to save his life. He was reared in a foreign household and though he lived his life as an Egyptian, he was not.

One day, Moses encountered two Hebrew men in an argument. He intervened and ended up killing one of them. When his actions were revealed, he fled for his life. Moses began a new life in a faraway place, existing in relative obscurity. He married a wife, had children, and established a routine. He likely even became comfortable and forgot the nagging "purpose ache" he had felt in his soul.

But Moses' God had not forgotten. He had not forgotten why He created Moses, and He has not forgotten you. There, on the backside of a mountain, God interrupted

Moses' life to get His attention. The Sovereign Ruler of the universe came down in the form of a burning bush to ignite a flame in Moses' soul. He came to remind him that he had a destiny.

On some level, we are all acquainted with the "purpose ache"--that aching feeling that we haven't scratched the surface of what our live is meant to be. Perhaps you have gotten off track or are facing very difficult circumstances that are blocking your view. Maybe you think it's too late, you're too old, or too much time has passed. Nothing could be further from the truth! When you feel like all of your dreams have died, you are the perfect candidate for an encounter with God. You are positioned to experience the Burning Bush.

The Burning Bush signifies the presence of God. We connect with the Burning Bush when God interrupts our lives to introduce us to our destiny. He begins to unravel the purpose for many of our life experiences. He gives language to the pain we have endured and uncovers its value. In that moment, He awakens our gifts and talents and begins to shed light on His plan for us.

Connecting with the Burning Bush signifies the convergence of your dreams with God's destiny for your life. In that moment, God gets your attention. He changes the trajectory of what your life will look like as you move forward. You finally begin to understand the purpose behind the painful events of your life and things you didn't quite understand. Through this new revelation, God exposes a new dimension of His character and unlocks your potential and purpose. More importantly, He invites you to join Him on an adventure—to partner with Him in transforming the world.

Because of His intervention, there is a simultaneous intersection of who you were, who you are, and who you are going to be. God reveals Himself as the God of your destiny and the Lover of your Soul. He breathes life into your dreams and convinces you that you are capable of accomplishments far greater than you ever envisioned.

At first, the vision will seem impossible, but it will begin to unfold with each small step of obedience. You do not want to miss this important appointment on your destiny calendar. Everything changes when you "Connect with the Burning Bush."

4

1.   BIRTH PAINS

WHOSE HAND ARE YOU HOLDING DURING THE STORMS OF LIFE?

My childhood was pretty normal. I grew up in a small town in northeastern Georgia, and I was raised in a two parent home. I had an older sister and brother who treated me like the stereotypical little sister. My mom cooked dinner five nights a week; on Saturday we went to McDonalds, and on Sunday she cooked her signature staple—roast beef with gravy, candied carrots, mashed potatoes, green beans, and cornbread. Every Sunday most of our extended family came over after church to get a plate.

We were a middle-class family. We had enough to live on, but not a lot of extras. My aunt and uncle lived next door, so my cousins, siblings, and I were raised together. We played on water slides, had pogo sticks, and an Atari. We had a babysitter who watched us after school so we wouldn't be "latchkey" kids. In the summer, we went to the library to read books and "picked and broke" green beans from my granddaddy's garden. We ate popsicles, Sugar Babies, and Pixie Sticks, and we walked around the neighborhood, free to play until the streetlights came on.

On Sundays, we went to church. When church was over, we went home for dinner, and then we went to church again—usually an afternoon program or choir anniversary. I also went to Sunday school. That is how I learned most of the Bible stories I know today. Church attendance was always mandatory.

My siblings and I often made jokes about different preachers over the years. Although many of them preached moving sermons, there was rarely any discussion about how to live the Christian life. Yes, there were talks about the cross and salvation and heaven, but very little emphasis on the here and now. Worse still, I don't remember anyone preaching about having an intimate relationship with God or how to discover what God wanted from me after salvation.

My early training was focused more on religion and regimen than relationship. That paradigm set the stage for an awkward tension that existed for much of my childhood and young adult life. As I matured, I continued to attend church, but God was more like a thing to me than a person. I prayed, paid tithes, and did all the things "good Christians" are supposed to do. Still, I had no real connection with God. I had been taught, albeit subconsciously, that avoiding the list of "thy shalt not's" was the purpose of the Christian life. I was supposed to avoid God's judgment, but I learned nothing about why I should obey Him. No one at church talked about falling in love with Him.

The objective seemed only to try to keep God from being mad at me. Therefore, I did what was expected: I came to the altar, joined the church, and got baptized, but not much else changed. I guess you could say Jesus was my "Savior." I had made a confession of faith, so I was going to heaven. The "Lord" issue, however, was a different matter altogether. I was in control of all of my decisions. I called the shots, and I made the rules . . . or so I thought. It was easy to put God in a box, a safe place where He could be available as I needed him, but where He could do nothing to alter my life or make me uncomfortable. I was perfectly okay with this arrangement, but apparently He was not. My life began to unravel, and I began to realize that God as I knew Him was about to change.

My paternal grandfather and I were very close. He took me fishing with him until I refused to stop talking, and he drove me for rides around town. He really spoiled me. He came to pick me up almost every week. After he took me fishing, we always stopped by Dairy Queen for a vanilla cone. I also have him to thank for the extensive dental work I have.

I was a chewing gum addict. Whenever I ran out, I would have a huge fit. I would roll around on the floor, cry, and act really crazy. If it was nighttime, my parents would often refuse to go to the store. I was unfazed by their refusal, however, because I had an alternative plan. I would sneak into my bedroom and call my granddad. In thirty minutes or less, the doorbell would ring. My dad would answer the door and chide my grandfather for spoiling me. His rebuke never mattered. My granddad would brush right past him and come looking for me. I'd run to him, giggle with delight, and hug him real tight as he spun me around. That was my granddad, Juicy Fruit in tow!

As I grew older, our relationship remained close. I always came to visit my grandparents whenever I was home from college. One weekend there was a big party scheduled on campus. My friends and I chose our outfits and started planning early in the week. On Wednesday, my dad called to tell me that my grandfather was very sick. He suggested that I come home. I hate to admit it, but I grappled with the decision for a few hours. I pondered whether I should miss the party and drive home or give an excuse, pray for my grandfather and attend the party of the year.

Thankfully, I made the right decision; I went home. My grandfather was suffering from severe bronchitis; he struggled to breathe. Nevertheless, he was happy to see me and I spent some time with him in his room. My grandfather's illness was one of the first times that I saw my father broken. He wasn't very optimistic about my grandfather's recovery. The next week, after I returned to school, my grandfather passed away. I kept telling myself that I should be grateful since some people don't even get to meet their grandparents, but that did little to console me.

I was also extremely close to my grandmother. She played an integral part in my childhood and upbringing. Their house was directly behind ours through a little path. I loved taking the little path out back to have some of her homemade biscuits with jelly. They were so good! Sometimes she'd even have the bologna with the red rim around it. She let me fry some myself, and I'd laugh when the meat plopped up on its side when it was done.

My grandmother used Noxzema, and her skin was flawless. She also kept her furniture covered with the original plastic. It burned my legs when I sat on it in the summer. Her laughter was infectious. Her entire body would shake whenever she found something really funny. Every Thanksgiving she cooked dinner for our entire family. The food was good: dressing, ham, turkey, collard greens, macaroni and cheese, potato salad with paprika, and coconut cake—the whole shebang. There was a unique irony, though. When it was time to eat, she never would. She always said she was too tired to eat. I never quite understood how you could be too tired to eat until I got older and actually started cooking. On more than one occasion, I have prepared a huge dinner for others, watched everyone enjoy the meal, and then head out to get something for myself just like my grandmother used to.

Two years after my grandfather's death, my grandmother was found lifeless on her bedroom floor. The weirdest part about her death was that I had just seen her earlier that day. I went by to see her and she told me she was skipping church because her chest was hurting. I suggested that she go to the doctor, but she refused, insisting that it was just a little cough. Later, when I returned from church, we joked and laughed about her refusal to let me sit on her lap. I can still hear her contagious laughter as she jokingly pushed me onto the floor.

That night, I returned to college and settled in to finish my homework. Around 9:30, my phone rang. There was no caller ID at the time, so I had no idea who was on the other line. It was my mom. I could tell by her voice that something was wrong. She tried to make small talk and then she asked if I was alone. After a few minutes, she told me that my grandmother passed away. The revelation was so unexpected; I just held the phone for a minute. After asking if I was okay, she put my dad on the phone. He was still in shock too, so our conversation was brief.

Our family made it through those two losses, but our faith suffered a tremendous blow. We were all shaken. At the funeral and even in our home, everyone talked about God, but somehow this all made me wonder what He could possibly be doing. Even though we were all devastated, no one really talked about confronting God. I knew I was just expected to move forward, so I tried to.

Just as we were settling into our routines, tragedy struck again. My maternal grandmother's breast cancer returned, and it was spreading. She had been diagnosed with cancer many years before, but the cancer had gone into remission. News of the cancer's return was devastating. What had we done wrong? Why were we losing the matriarchs and patriarchs in our family? Was God punishing us? I was very confused.

I was home for the summer, so I agreed to take my grandmother to her weekly appointments at the cancer center. The trips back and forth to Anderson, S.C. were memorable. We talked about cooking, church, and boys! She had so much wisdom to share. I had to get most of my questions and conversations out on the way there, though. On the way back, she was always tired and grouchy. The treatments were grueling and they didn't appear to be helping. In fact, her condition seemed to be getting worse.

One day, my aunt brought her an herb called wormwood. My grandmother took it, and passed something that looked alive in her stool. My aunt called it the "mother" parasite, and everyone was really excited. Everyone, that is, except my grandmother. The "mother" scared her so bad that she refused to take any more. We begged her to let the herb do its job, but she refused. Sadly, her body continued to weaken.

In late December, she called us all together for a family meeting. She had an announcement to make. She told us rather emphatically that she would not be around for Christmas. She said she was not going to ruin it for us. We all cried and begged her not to say she was dying. We assured her that she was not a burden. We wanted her to stay. She was resolute. She said she was going home to be with Jesus.

Later that week, as my sister and mother sat by her bedside, the light fixture began to shine brightly. Almost on cue, my grandmother began looking into the light. She started talking to someone, but she was not addressing either of them. She prayed for every member of our family, one by one, asking God to bless us. At the end, she told God she was ready to go home. She also called out to her mother and father and pleaded with them not to leave her. She said she wanted to go with them. Apparently, their answer was, "no," because the light returned to normal, and she silently lay back on the bed.

Though there was no doubt that something supernatural occurred, my grandmother said she hadn't been talking to anyone. Two days later, she passed away. Her death signaled a significant change in my life. In a matter of three short years, I had only one grandparent left. I had known and enjoyed the protection and love of my grandparents for my entire life. Their deaths dramatically shifted our familial interactions; my extended family didn't get together nearly as often and we started drifting apart. All these transitions prompted me to begin some serious soul searching.

Developing my own relationship with God happened slowly over the next few years as I entered real adulthood. I prayed more and even found a church I enjoyed. It was very strange at first. A lot of what I thought I knew about God was largely untrue. I thought He was just waiting for me to do something wrong so he could "ping" me, so coming close to him was almost impossible. I also had a much deeper issue that made it difficult for us to connect. I was afflicted with the "orphan spirit." Orphans don't have parents. They are disconnected from their history which impacts and shapes their identity. They spend much of their life trying to search for significance and acceptance, never really feeling like they are loved just for who they are. When I heard a sermon on the subject at church, God began to unveil darkness in my soul. Its existence was a truth I wasn't quite prepared to accept.

I had been raised to follow strict guidelines of behavior. As a consequence, I thought I had to earn God's love. Somewhere deep inside I didn't believe that God inherently loved me irrespective of my behavior. I didn't think that I was worthy of love merely by virtue of the fact that I existed. That false belief kept me on a path of works and religion, trying hard not to mess things up. Whenever I

11

failed, I felt rejected and unloved. It would take years and many seasons of healing before that ever changed.

It did not help that I came from two very driven parents. My father was a self-taught custom cabinet builder, and my mother was a customer service representative for the electric company and a city councilwoman. She was the first African-American to be elected to the city council in my predominately white and decidedly traditional Southern town. Surprisingly, she ran a successful campaign with the simple slogan, "Please give me a chance!" It is even more surprising that she ran, unopposed, for thirty years until her retirement.

Neither of my parents graduated from college, but my mother graduated from high school when she was 16. She was class valedictorian. My mom went to business school for one semester before learning that she was pregnant. Her husband was also in college, so a choice had to be made. As was consistent for that time period, she had to drop out and stay home.

My father went to the Army after high school and served in Vietnam. He served for four years before he returned. He never really got over some of his experiences in Vietnam. His MOS (Military Occupational Specialty) was tagging the bodies of the deceased soldiers for their return to the United States. Even though it had been almost 40 years, he said that the smell of the burning flesh was still in his nostrils. His time in Vietnam haunted him, even in his dreams. Many days, as he lay peacefully napping in the chair, he would suddenly be struck with a memory. He would start kicking the ground, groaning, and wake up abruptly. He often dreamt of dogs attacking him while he slept. When winter began each year, his disposition took a very dramatic turn. He rarely wanted to go anywhere. He preferred to stay at home, all day, sitting in his favorite chair. It wasn't until much later that I was able to convince him to seek treatment at the Veterans Administration. He was diagnosed with depression, post-traumatic disorder, and some other medical issues that were a direct result of the Agent Orange that was used in Vietnam.

Though neither of my parents had college degrees, not attending was not an option for us. From the very beginning of our schooling, it was clearly understood. We were expected to excel in school, graduate, attend college, obtain a college degree, and get a great job. Those expectations were non-negotiable. While their lofty ideals for our lives were admirable, they also created a level of perfectionism that would prove to be very unhealthy.

I graduated from college and quickly landed a job. I was offered my first teaching job at our college job fair during the spring. I began the school year as a 22 year old, first year teacher. I taught high school juniors and seniors, so many of my students were 18 years old themselves. I set strict standards for my students, and they failed to meet them. Because of my upbringing and driven personality, I was unyielding. The end of term failing grades created a firestorm in the small town.

Even though most of my students were black, my colleagues were not. The principal visited my classroom. Other teachers visited my classroom. All of them came to the same conclusions. My pedagogy was flawless, yet the parents of many of my students were furious. The HOPE scholarship (a scholarship funded from the lottery that was based on a student's G.P.A.) was in full swing. There was an apparent conflict of interest. My focus was on student preparation; the parents' bottom line was their children's grades. The disgruntled parents lined the halls on parent conference night, and many of them removed their students from my class.

Finally, the superintendent had enough. He paid my classroom a visit. After his evaluation, he came to see me. He praised my teaching style, my presentation, even my ability to keep the students engaged. After a few moments of conversation, he leaned back in his chair and just looked at me. I nervously anticipated what he would say next. "Ms. Mayfield?" he asked, "You do know why you are getting all this backlash from your students' parents don't you?" I honestly had to reply that I did not. He continued, "It's because you're black. White people don't believe that a black person can speak proper English, much less teach it." He could tell by my face that I was stunned. He continued, "You must know that. I cannot speak against anything I observed in your classroom, but that doesn't mean the people here will ever accept it."

I couldn't believe what I was hearing. I would not say that I lived a sheltered life. I had always been in the minority, but my parents worked very hard to make me believe that I was equal to everyone else. They always told me that if I got an education and worked really hard, doors of opportunity would fly open for me. The superintendent's words suggested that their lofty ideals would not be applicable here.

Needless to say, the year was tumultuous. At the end of the school year I moved to another district, then to another at the end of the following year. I knew I was called to be a teacher, but I could not seem to find my niche. Most of my students were performing far below their grade levels, but I could not find an administration that seemed dedicated to changing that reality. Worse still, I was ostracized by my colleagues for "causing problems." Most of them couldn't understand why I wouldn't just go with the status quo and give students good grades.

I was frustrated and discouraged, but the thought never occurred to me to change my standards. I had just left college, so I was well acquainted with the expectations and rigor that awaited my students. Finally, one of my colleagues expressed what I was slowly beginning to recognize. He told me that college preparatory classes weren't really preparation for college. The classes were really just a label to make parents feel prestigious!

At that, I decided to move back to my hometown where I was hired as a middle school assistant principal. I was the first African-American to serve there in that capacity, and I was aware of that fact on a daily basis. There were about 72 teachers in my school, and only two of them were black. The custodial staff, however, was all black except for one. Surprisingly, the sole Caucasian custodian came to be my closest ally on the entire staff. As it turns out, he knew my mother from her work at the electricity company and city government. He was very fond of her integrity and fairness. Throughout all the difficulty, adversity, and mistreatment I suffered, he always encouraged me.

Many of the teachers I supervised had been my teachers when I was in school. They were not very happy having me as their supervisor. I was young, 26 at the time, intelligent, and black. On almost a daily basis there was a challenge to my authority. I found little solace with my principal. He urged me to foster relationships with the teachers, but my efforts were met with stiff opposition. They did not want relationship; they wanted a white supervisor. Most of the teachers made it obvious that they did not want me as their leader.

The year ended on a very climatic note. In my year end evaluation meeting, I questioned the validity of the scores and the method my principal used for my evaluation. He began screaming, lunged across his desk, and I ended up running out of his office. Later, the superintendent changed my evaluation, but my principal refused to have me in "his"

15

school anymore. After a very contentious meeting among the three of us, I was offered the opportunity to resign in lieu of non-renewal. I refused, standing firm in the fact that I had done nothing wrong. As a result, my contract was not renewed.

I ended up filing a federal lawsuit against the school system. It was the premier topic of conversation for everyone in the small town I called home. Some of the most painful events of my life happened during that period. I had already lost so much. I knew I had done a great job, just like with my first year of teaching. Nevertheless, I was out of a job . . . again. My brother-in-law was on the school board, but he did nothing to help. He remained silent on the issue at home, but I always suspected that he shared some of the items we discussed among our family with the members of the board.

My aunt was also an administrator at the board office. During depositions for the case, she repeatedly lied under oath. It was so bad that my attorney requested a recess to ask me if I was okay. By that time, I was numb. I told him, "I'm fine. If she has decided to lie, so be it. Show no mercy." I prepared a list of questions for him to ask. By the end of her deposition, it was obvious to everyone in the room that she was lying. Even though that was an apparent victory, it provided no consolation for me. She was my aunt. She was my mom's sister. She had changed my diapers and babysat me when I was small. She even took me to get my ears pierced when I was a baby. Her brazen betrayal broke me.

I drove home in silence. When I arrived, my dad was sitting in his Lazy Boy chair. I ran to him and perched heavily on his lap. Though I was fully a woman, one who stands almost 6'0 tall, I wanted nothing more than to be a little girl again. I did not want to "adult" anymore.

I filled his shirt with my tears. "She lied, Dad, she lied! How could she do this to me?" He lifted my head and looked into my eyes. "Adrienne, everyone isn't as strong as you. It takes courage to stand up for what is right. It will all be okay." I wasn't so sure that his words were true, but hearing them provided temporary relief for the raging war in my soul.

As I tried to find other witnesses to bolster my case, support began to wane. People who said they stood with me started to drop like flies. One day, the custodian who had been my biggest cheerleader came to see me at my parent's house. When I opened the door, his countenance fell. He asked if he could talk with me, so I stepped outside. He said that while he knew what happened was wrong, he was asking me not to involve him. He had been diagnosed with cancer and he needed his health insurance. He knew his support of me could cost him his job. He wanted to be sure I would not ask him to testify or answer any questions. I tried to keep a straight face and choke back the tears that were welling up inside my throat. Instead of expressing my disappointment, I told him I understood his situation and gave him a hug. After all, this was MY fight. I couldn't expect anyone else to join my cause, could I? After he left, I went inside and cried. . . again.

We continued with depositions and preparation for the case. The bills were mounting and I had to produce the money upfront. My parents contributed to the cause and my brother wrote a check, too, but the expenses were pushing me to drop the case. Most civil rights cases struggle to make it past summary judgment, so I knew that filing the response was very important. On the weekend before my summary judgment response was due, my attorney was arrested for a domestic dispute. One of my cousins sent me a copy of the newspaper article. Now I knew why he hadn't taken my calls.

Everything that could go wrong was headed in that direction. I had to petition the court for an extension. Thankfully, his wife assisted me with completing the response.

The court granted the school board's motion for summary judgment. Unless I decided to file an appeal, the case was over. Just like that. I had a decision to make. I had already spent over $20,000 fighting this injustice. I talked with my parents about dropping the case. They told me I had their support with whatever I decided. I couldn't let them continue to invest their money, and I didn't want to spend my entire savings fighting to remain in a place where I wasn't wanted. I chose not to appeal.

I moved to Atlanta the following year. There were no administrative vacancies at the time, so I headed back into the classroom. Things went well. I was in a newly built school and my principal was highly skilled at running a tight ship. He was a true leader and his commitment to excellence pushed us all to work hard to educate the students in our classrooms. After I had been there for two years, I started to settle in.

On Super Bowl weekend that year, I went home and my Dad kept complaining about his hip. I remember him getting on the floor writhing in pain. I thought he was joking, so I put my foot on him. He groaned, and I finally realized he was serious. I tried to get him to go to the hospital, but he said he'd give it "a few days."

I returned back to Atlanta and checked in with my mom through the week. My father wasn't getting better, so they decided to travel to Augusta to the VA hospital. The doctors there said he was severely constipated, so they prescribed medication and released him. My parents returned home, but nothing alleviated the pain. I felt like I needed to intervene, so I went home again. He was not getting any better. My mom and I finally managed to convince him to go back to the hospital.

I wanted desperately to make the drive with them to Augusta. Unfortunately, my parents decided to go alone. I couldn't understand why I had to stay behind. I was starting to feel scared, and I needed them to comfort me and assure me that everything was fine. No assurance would come. They left, asking me to stay and manage affairs at home.

I will never forget what happened as my mom and I walked my dad to the door. He looked back at me and said, "I expect you to take care of your sister and brother." I protested, "What are you talking about? But I'm the youngest! Besides, nothing is going to happen to you. You're going to be fine." He didn't respond. As I watched them drive away, my eyes filled with tears. What was happening? My mom and dad were leaving for the hospital and I was at home, all alone. I quietly closed the door and went to sit on the sofa. I wanted to pray, but I didn't really know what to say. I just sat there and wept. I could sense a definitive shift in that moment. My life was changing . . . again.

I returned to Atlanta and waited for an update from my mom. My mom kept insisting that the doctors check his appendix, but they dismissed her request. Three years prior, my father had become deathly ill and had emergency surgery. The gastroenterologist intended to remove his appendix, but the area was highly inflamed and infected. He cleared as much as he could and told my father to return for removal in a few months. My dad never went back, but he had the incision from the procedure. Because of the incision, the doctors dismissed my mom's suggestion that the issue might be his appendix. They kept insisting that he did not have one.

A ruptured appendix is extremely serious because the

rupture spreads bacteria and fecal matter into the abdomen. If it is not addressed immediately, it can be fatal. By the time the doctors took the time to verify my mother's diagnosis, it was too late. My father's body had become septic. The poison had spread throughout his body. The doctors wouldn't let us give him anything to eat or drink though he begged for just a sip of water. They were treating him with the strongest antibiotics available, but his white blood count continued to elevate.

The following Sunday, I could tell my mom was getting weary. I told her we should go to church. She hesitated at first, but she finally conceded. She went in to talk to my dad and promised him we'd be back as soon as church was over. As I looked into the door, I saw a look in my dad's eyes that I still remember. I could feel a yawning chasm begin to open between us. He sat up and looked at me in the doorway, but he remained silent. I wanted to run to him, but something stopped me. It was like I was paralyzed. I couldn't move. We locked eyes for about ten seconds, and I walked away.

My mom and I went to church and came back as soon as it was over. Nothing prepared us for what we found waiting for us. As we prepared to walk down the hall to his room, the nurse appeared. She said the doctor needed to speak with us. We suggested he meet us in my dad's room because we had promised to come back soon. She refused. She seated us in a waiting area and the doctor came in. He told us that they had decided to put my father on a ventilator. Without a phone call. Without consent. They had already done it. The doctor maintained that it was just to give my dad's body a rest since it had been working so hard to fight the infection, but something in my gut told me different.

For the next four days, we sat anxiously by his bed

hoping and praying for improvement in his condition, but none came. His white blood count remained high and all his vital signs were at dangerous levels. I prayed; I cried; I begged God for mercy.

I was not ready for my father to die. I was only 33. I had always envisioned growing old with my parents, not without them. One night, after sitting at the hospital all night, my siblings, mom, and I finally decided to head to our hotel. We stopped by IHOP, had a late dinner and headed "home." Just as we headed upstairs to ready for bed, the phone rang. It was the hospital. They told us that my father had "taken a turn for the worse." They wanted us to come back to the hospital. We were exhausted. I looked over at the clock. It was 1:30 a.m.

I remember looking at my mom's face. She looked much older and very weary. I told her not to worry; I would drive. When we arrived, the doctor brought all of us into a room and said that my father's oxygen levels were decreasing. He told us we could go in to see him, but we would need to make a decision about what we wanted to do. We headed down the hall and my mom stopped midway. She leaned onto the wall and said, "I can't do this. I can't walk down this hall again to look at him like this." My brother told her she didn't have to; we would go. My siblings and I paused for a moment and walked ahead. When we looked back, my mom was slowly walking behind us.

As much as I wanted to deny it, when I looked at father I knew he was leaving. He was connected to so many machines and his breathing was very rattled. We each told him how much we loved him. My mom spoke lovingly to him, and I begged him to come back to us. There was no response from him, but we hoped and prayed that he could somehow hear us. As we exited the room, my mom told the doctor that if my dad's heart stopped again, they should attempt resuscitation. After that attempt, if it failed again, they should allow him to go in peace. Almost as soon as she said the words, the machines tying my father to this world started going crazy, and we were quickly ushered to the waiting room.

Many images of life with my dad flashed through my mind. When I was small, we made almost daily runs to Dairy Queen. I enjoyed a vanilla cone; his sweet selection was always a banana split. He was the one who usually disciplined me. He was the one who gave my dates "the talk" so that they were too scared to even move. He was also the one who taught me how to perfect the form of my free throw shot, and he was the one who required that my bed was made every morning, and that the water was not left running while I brushed my teeth. My dad was such an integral part of my growth as a child and adult. I was completely unprepared to even consider living life without him.

None of us talked as we sat there. We were really trying to process it all. A few minutes later, my head fell backward, and I began speaking in tongues. It was totally involuntary. As a matter of fact, I had only recently received the baptism of the Holy Spirit. I was raised in a very traditional Baptist church. No one really talked about the supernatural. Dancing, speaking in tongues, and prophesy were all things reserved for the "holiness" church down the street. I was an adult before I learned that holiness is a lifestyle not a denomination. Holiness is the commitment to living a life being set apart and separate. It actually is required by everyone who says they believe in God, not just a particular denomination.

My prayer language went on for about two minutes. It was like an out of body experience. I could hear myself speaking, but I had no control over what I was saying. I heard my sister whisper, "She's arguing with God." Suddenly, my head fell forward, and I let out a loud exhale. Less than thirty seconds later, the doctor came to the door to tell us my father was gone.

My family all went to my father's room and stood around the bed. It was very bizarre. For the first time in days, I could feel my father's presence in the room. Though his body lay in front of me on the hospital bed, I somehow knew his soul was no longer in there. I could feel his spirit in the room: I knew it wasn't in his body. Suddenly, I felt a strong desire to sing a hymn. I told my family we should sing "Amazing Grace" since my father was being escorted into heaven. The doctors all stood there, speechless. One of the interns started to cry. We sang through a chorus or two. God was there in the room. I could feel a sustaining strength overtaking me. I knew it was not my own.

We prayed and stoically walked from the hospital room. My brother stayed close to my mom. We all wanted to make sure she was okay. The four of us stayed in a hotel for a few hours. We were supposed to be sleeping, but that didn't happen. There were too many phone calls and too much restless energy among us. As soon as day broke, we checked out and drove four separate cars, following each other, back to my hometown.

When we arrived, people were waiting for us at my parent's house. It didn't matter. There was much work to be done. My mother told us she wanted arrangements handled quickly, so I went inside to find a suit. Within three days, we laid my father to rest and I, again, tried to make sense of my life.

The grief and trauma was shared by all of us, but it had the most profound effect on my mom. She and my father had been inseparable. They did everything together

Connecting With The Burning Bush

once my mother retired. They took joy rides every night around 12:30 a.m. The local police joked with my mom that third shift knew to expect my dad's white truck to show up late at night cruising through town. They enjoyed choosing flowers for their garden and picking peaches and muscadines. Theirs was the epitome of retirement life. I knew I would have to find a way to fill the void for my mom; I COULD NOT lose her too.

2. SPIRITUAL WARFARE BOOTCAMP

HOW DOES GOD TRAIN ME TO FIGHT?

My father's death was catastrophic for all of us. It was so unexpected; it caught us completely off guard. I tried to stay close to my mom because of the gravity of her loss. We adapted very slowly but tried to move forward. In December 2008, our family gathered at my brother's house to celebrate Christmas. Somehow we got into a heated debate, and my brother demanded that we all leave his house. It was almost midnight, so it was difficult for all of us to find a place to go.

I had been praying for my brother's spiritual transformation, but these events made me feel like my prayers were not reaching past the ceiling. He was becoming someone I did not know. The following February, I received a call from him late in the night. He was acting very strange. He started talking about going to jail and how people had planted chips into his brain. Nothing he was saying was making any sense. I tried praying. I tried talking. I tried to calm him, but nothing was working. I knew that I needed help, so I called my mom on three-way. She tried talking to him. He became more and more belligerent. We started praying for him, but he was not responding. Something diabolical had taken hold of him, and it was not letting him go.

Just as my mom and I started praying again, he dropped the phone. When I tried to call him back, he did not answer. I was very worried. I knew he was visiting a

25

friend's house, but I did not know how to get there. I called my mother back and we prayed together. We both decided that we would have to trust God with him. We had no clue where he was, so we were left with no other option. I finally fell asleep around 2 a.m.

I was awakened around 9:00 a.m. by a frantic phone call. My brother's boyfriend was on the other line, telling me that they could not find him. My brother had walked out of the house after our phone call the previous night. He left his car keys, wallet, and identification behind. He left on foot, and no one had heard from him. Though he had been gone for hours, his friends had not called the police. I was furious! I immediately hung up and looked for the phone number. My heart was beating out of my chest, but my adrenaline had also kicked in. I called the Alpharetta police department and told them what I knew. The officer said he would call me back if he received any details. In the meantime, I called my mom and caught her up to speed on what I'd learned. As soon as I hung up the phone with my mom, my phone rang. It was the policeman.

"Ms. Mayfield, hello, this is Officer Smith. We found your brother."

Not again.

"Found?" Wait, what could that mean? Was my brother dead too?

I wanted to drop the phone and run. Instead, I breathed deeply, and he continued, "We found him. We have taken him to Grady Hospital. He did not have any identification, so you will need to go to the hospital as soon as possible with his ID so the hospital knows who he is. Right now he is admitted as John Doe." I thanked him for the information and immediately called my mom. It would take her and my sister two hours to reach Atlanta, so I had to go to the hospital alone. I also had to ask his boyfriend to meet me there since he had my brother's wallet and ID. I drove to the hospital, thinking about my life. I had a Valentine's date that night. It had been a while since I had just done anything fun—just let my hair down. Well, obviously that wouldn't be happening. I scrambled to find my friend's number and called him on the way to the hospital. He started asking me a million questions, and I could not take it. My stress level was out the roof. I'm pretty sure I just hung up on him.

I had no idea what I was going to find at the hospital, and I was scared. There was no one to support me, again. I parked my car and walked inside slowly. I had to complete an endless amount of paperwork and answer lots of questions. Finally, after what felt like hours, I was finally allowed to see my brother.

When I walked into the room, I fell backward. He was restrained in the bed, and his eyes were taped shut. His eyelids were as huge as baseballs. Seeing him this way was surreal. The doctor reached for my arm, trying to stabilize me. He asked me if I was okay. I remember saying, "No, I am not. But I will be." His boyfriend came rushing into the room and began sobbing uncontrollably. I went over to comfort him. I went over to comfort HIM. I was distraught. I looked down at my brother. He was obviously wounded and traumatized, yet I was expected to comfort his boyfriend. No one was there to comfort me.

The doctor began to share the details of my brother's condition and prognosis. He had been placed in a medically induced coma because he arrived so irate. It had taken five police officers to restrain him. Looking back, I am even more grateful for God's grace in this situation. In recent encounters with black men and police officers, confrontations have usually ended with someone being dead. My brother is a 6'2 black man who weighs over 350 pounds.

His episode occurred in a very affluent, predominantly white suburb outside Atlanta. His situation could easily have turned out even more tragically had it not been for God's grace and mercy.

My mother and sister arrived, and they went in to see him. I had to fill them in on the details and we also had to make decisions about who was going to stay with him. Thankfully, I remembered that one of my close friends worked at Grady. Providentially, he was the charge nurse on my brother's floor! His presence meant that we could go home and get a few hours of sleep. We should never despair, even when we are overwhelmed. God always has a ram in the bush!

For the next five days, I encountered intense spiritual warfare. Each time I went in to see my brother, he would manifest a nature other than his own. At times his voice would deepen, his eyes would turn blood-shot red and he would warn us to leave. His behavior was like something people watch in a Freddy Krueger film. The voices I heard and the things he said were not coming from him. If we stayed despite his warnings, he would say he could not be responsible for what happened to us. Then he would transition and begin talking normally, trying to tell us what happened to him. Every time he tried to share the events, he would start to cry. It was clear that he had endured something very traumatic.

We continued to pray for him day and night. I obtained permission to place a CD player in his hospital room. Scriptures and worship music played in his room 24/7. My mom and I alternated sitting with him. She sat with him all day while I tried to work. I came right after school and stayed throughout the night. Looking back on the experience, I know it was only God that sustained me.

Finally after about 12 days in the hospital, the doctors

decided it was time to release him. They wanted to transfer him to a psychiatric hospital a 48 hour evaluation. I was supposed to stay with him until then so my mother could get some extra rest. As I sat by his bed, listening to the Christian music I had put in his room, I began to minister to him. I told him that I understood he had been through something terrible. We could talk about all of it later. The important thing at this point, though, was making a definite decision for Jesus Christ. Jesus had rescued him from a near-death experience. Now it was his turn to do something for Him. My brother needed to surrender his life to Jesus. I paused and waited for his response. He was quiet for a few moments, and then he said, "I'm ready! I want Jesus in my life. He came to rescue me." As he spoke, tears rolled down his cheeks. His heart was tender toward God. He was ready. We got down on our knees, there in his hospital room, and held hands. I led him in a prayer to receive Jesus Christ as his Savior. Hallelujah!

The psychiatric hospital only kept him for 24 hours. Fourteen days after this horrific ordeal began, my brother was released. We decided that he would go home to my mother's house. He was afraid to be at his house alone. I was nervous for my mom to be alone with him, but I had to work, and I lived two hours away. I promised my mom I would come home every weekend and provide her some relief.

My life would have to wait. My family needed me. It was a very tough process. He often had nightmares and my mom didn't get much sleep, but we didn't give up. I drove home every weekend for three months. We kept praying, and God was faithful. He saved my brother and put him on the path to becoming a brand new man!

Our family experienced so many traumatic events back to back; it was very hard to rebound. It is worth stating, though, that God's grace was tremendous during this period. I learned to trust Him completely because there were many days when I knew I could not go forward otherwise. Although trauma and grief are common to all, learning to master them is a balancing act. No one escapes them completely unscathed, but you can make it through if you rely on a God who is able to handle everything. Without Him, a series of traumatic events can easily immobilize you for years. Thankfully, all the adversity had taught me to walk closely with God. His stability made all the difference.

The following year, my mom came to visit me one weekend. I went to lunch with one of my friends, and my mom called to say she planned to call 911. She had been struggling with diarrhea for a few days, but I didn't think it was anything serious. I told her to wait for a few minutes, so I could come take her.

We arrived at the hospital and she was quickly admitted. Her white blood count was extremely elevated, so they began searching for an infection. Not . . . again. Thankfully, she was admitted in the hospital right next door to the high school where I taught. I was getting dangerously close to having no available leave with all the calamity our family had endured.

For twelve days, the doctors, specialists, and nurses poked, prodded, and tested my mom, but they were stumped. She would eat her food, but everything she ate just passed through. Still, the doctors had no medical diagnosis to support her condition. Her body was obviously under attack by something very aggressive. They experimented with numerous antibiotics to see if her body would respond. Finally she began to improve, but she wasn't totally healed. I had a strong suspicion that her illness was connected to my father's death. Though she was verifiably ill, no medical diagnosis was ever given.

Still, the doctors decided to send her home. They said that they had done all they knew to do. I told my mom she would have to stay with me for a week until we were sure she was better. She resisted, but I didn't budge. There was no way I could go home to be with her, and there was no one else. I had to work, and her house was two hours away. She finally agreed. In a week, she was better, so I was able to take her home.

She slowly improved and returned back to normal. Despite all these challenges, I continued to teach. By then, I was pretty much a pro. Though I tried to keep my instruction interesting, I was getting disgruntled with my results. My students were underperforming, availability of resources was limited, and I knew I was becoming stagnant as an individual. I was a great teacher; I loved my students, but I wasn't growing anymore. I wasn't being challenged. I had lost my passion for teaching. I knew I had to do something.

3.   THE STRIPPING

HOW DO YOU RESPOND WHEN
GOD'S ANSWER IS "NO?"

When Congress passed the No Child Left Behind Legislation, I was done. Government officials issued mandates for student performance, but they failed to provide resources for the tremendous divide between my students' literacy and their expectations of them. As I listened to their rhetoric, I realized that they were fishing in the dark. They weren't educators. They had no clue about the day to day operations of a school, yet they continued to pretend to know what they were doing. Their arrogance was nauseating.

Every day I was confronted with the pressure to get students to perform for tests and benchmarks that appeared beyond their capability. Frustration with my profession actually created the impetus for my next move. As I studied the people making the decisions, I had an epiphany. The people with a seat at the table were legislators. Most legislators were lawyers. If I wanted to contribute to the conversation, I needed to change my position. I needed to become a lawyer.

I had taken the LSAT a few years before, and it was brutal. There was no way I was going to sit through that exam again. I began researching the process for law admission and learned that my scores for most schools would expire that year. On a hope and a prayer, I began the admission process. I was accepted by several schools, but I decided the University of Georgia was the best choice. It was close to home, a great value, and ranked in the top 25 of Tier 1 schools. Going from teacher to student was quite a transition. I was 37 years old, and I hadn't been a student in 12 years! For the first time in my life, I found myself at the bottom of the grading curve. I started wondering if I had made the right decision.

Despite my slow start, I kept pushing. Second semester started and things were a little smoother. I began to get more comfortable with the Socratic Method. My mom encouraged me to persevere. We prayed every day and some weeks she'd drive to Athens to spend time with me. My mom and I talked on the telephone several times a day, but I began to notice that she didn't sound the same. When I confronted her, she told me that she was sick again. She was having trouble breathing. She hadn't told me because she didn't want me to worry and lose my focus on school.

She had already been to her family doctor, and he diagnosed her with asthma. I never accepted that diagnosis. My mom was 63. Surely if she was asthmatic, we'd known before then. She continued to complain, so my brother agreed to take off from his job to go home and check on her. The doctor dismissed her symptoms again, so they didn't make much progress. The doctor finally settled on a sleep apnea diagnosis and prescribed a C-Pap for her.

Her breathing issue continued to worsen, so on the Saturday before Easter I took her to the emergency room. The physician was ruthless and impatient. He told my mom the breathing issue was anxiety and instructed her to calm down. She started to cry. She couldn't breathe. His apathy infuriated me but I was powerless to influence a more thorough examination. He prescribed some anti-anxiety medication and released her.

The following Monday, I took her to her family doctor

in tears. The nurses immediately took her back to the examination room. Her doctor finally admitted that the issue was beyond his expertise. He referred her to another physician in a nearby city. We drove her there and they admitted her. They were able to get her breathing more under control with their version of her home C-PAP. It was much more powerful.

A few days later, the doctor came in to see us. He had a very grim look on his face. He said, "I'm not sure how to say this. When I received the initial test results, I did not want to believe them, so I sent the lab results to California for reevaluation. Ms. Mayfield, you have stage four breast cancer and it has begun to metastasize."

We were all speechless. My grandmother's death from breast cancer had heightened our family's awareness. My mom was diligent about her mammograms. She even worked for the district health department, training women on the importance of self-care and monthly breast exams. As a matter of fact, my mom's last mammogram had been performed in October, not more than six months before. She had been given a normal result. Breast cancer had claimed the life of my grandmother. Now it was coming for my mother. How could this be happening?

There was no need arguing the diagnosis at this point. We had to discuss treatment options. The oncologist told us that my mother was a good candidate for radiation pills. If the radiation was successful, she would not need chemotherapy. He left the room. I wanted to throw up. I was nauseous. My head was spinning, and I wanted to cry. Though I felt all these emotions, I could not allow any of them to show. I had to be strong. My mom was counting on me. After a family discussion, we decided that she would go forward with the treatment.

I didn't know what any of this would mean for law

school. I was by no means at the top of my class, and final exams were fast approaching. I also had been offered a clerkship with a federal judge—a highly coveted summer position. No one in their right mind turned those down. Still, I knew there was no decision to be made. I would allow nothing to be placed before my commitment to my mother's care. I contacted all my professors and the dean and informed them about my situation. When I called the judge who had offered me the clerkship, she told me I should focus on my mom. I didn't even have to explain.

The radiation treatment went well, but they were not able to get my mom's breathing stabilized. They were already using a machine to pull the fluid, but it wasn't effective. The medical team decided to put talc inside my mother's lung to control the accumulating fluid. The whole idea of putting something in her lungs that would harden and be irreversible sounded questionable to me. I didn't like the sound of it. My spring semester writing prompt in law school was about a medical procedure where the patient's lung deflated during surgery; knowledge of that reality didn't inspire me with much confidence. Things didn't turn out well for the patient, so I was not in favor of the procedure. The doctors made it seem like that was really our only option, so my mom agreed.

The day of the surgery, the doctor came in and told me the operation would take about 45 minutes to complete. He explained the procedure again, and my mom seemed at peace with it. They prepared her for the surgery; we prayed together, and they wheeled her away.

An hour and a half later, my mom had not returned and there was no news. I began to call the nurses' station. I was frantic. They had no answers. I walked down the hall to find someone to help. They told me that they'd call me in a few minutes. I should just go back to the room and wait. When I returned to the room, they finally called. They told me there were some complications, but she was stable. Rather than being returned to the room, they were taking her to the intensive care unit.

After what seemed like hours they finally allowed me to see my mom. She was hooked up to all kinds of machines, and she looked very sick. When I approached her bed, she desperately grabbed my hand. She had such an intense fear in her eyes. "They tried to kill me. They tried to kill me. I almost died in there." I didn't know what to think. I tried to calm her. I wasn't sure who "they" were but I knew she needed to settle down. I told her everything would be okay. I promised not to leave her side.

A few minutes later, the nurse told me that there were some people outside who wanted to see her. I had no idea who it was, so I went out to see. All of my immediate family was gathered outside the intensive care unit! They were all asking to see Mom. She had just come out of a very traumatic surgery, and I needed to make sense of what she told me. Still, I knew it would not be good for me to deny them access, so I agreed. Two by two they filed into the room. I'm sure even if my mom had not already been thinking something was wrong, she did then. That many people only come to see someone when they are dying.

While they each went in to see her, I went to meet with the doctor. The actual surgeon refused to see me. He said he was going home! I was beyond upset, but I could not focus on him. I needed answers. The intensive care doctor agreed to talk to me, so I waited for him to come to the consultation room. He looked as though he had lost all hope. He told me that my mom was very sick and would likely not make it through the night. He suggested that we put her on a ventilator. A ventilator! No! Not again. I refused to give him consent. He looked me squarely in the eye and said, "Then you, my dear, have just signed your mother's death certificate. She will not make it through the night."

My aunts were standing near me and they suggested that I call for my brother and sister to get their opinion. My brother had been at the hospital with me earlier that day. We got into an argument about a phone call, and he left me at the hospital all alone, even though we had no answers about where Mom was. I refused their suggestion. I was resolute. I defiantly stared back at the doctor. "Sir, I respect your opinion, but life and death are in the hands of God. In the morning, my mother will still be alive and you will have a testament of the power of the God I serve!" He laughed at me and walked away. Something inside was telling me to trust God. Besides, my mother was already traumatized. I could not put her through another procedure.

The procession of sullen faces finally abated. As expected, my mom asked me if she was dying. She wanted to know why all those people were there. I told her everyone was just concerned about the surgery. I laid hands on her and prayed for peace. I had no doubt that God would answer my prayers and spare my mother's life. The next morning, she was still alive. She began to stabilize and after a few days, she was returned to a regular room. Her oncologist said she would need to wait a couple of days to resume the radiation treatment.

Over the next couple of weeks, my mother was transferred. I tried to fight the transfer, but the insurance regulations prevailed. She was sent to a rehabilitation facility. They were ill prepared to address my mom's care. They did not have her radiation therapy. In fact, I had to speak with the hospital administrator to finally get it. A full 48 hours passed without the radiation pill she desperately needed.

A couple of days later I went to the hospital. My mom was traumatized again. Earlier that day, when the nurses brought her back to her room, they forgot to plug in her oxygen machine. She kept telling them that she couldn't breathe, but she was ignored. It was 45 minutes before someone finally realized that the machine was not plugged in. I was beyond upset, but my mom begged me not to say anything. She told me if I made them angry, they might be mean to her when she was all alone. I reluctantly agreed, but started documenting all of their mishaps.

When I went to visit my mom the following Monday, they told me she was at occupational therapy. I thought that was a great idea, so I headed down to the room to see what she was doing. My mom was sitting at a table, surrounded by other patients doing a kindergarten coloring sheet! The page had a list of fruit and she had to circle the ones that began with the letter "A." I could not believe what I was seeing; there was nothing wrong with my mother's mental faculties! Why was she coloring and circling fruit? I had had enough of their incompetence. I wrote a scathing letter to the hospital administrator noting all of the events that occurred. The next day, my mom called me and told me to come get her. She said she was being "released." She joked that her "lawyer daughter" had gotten her kicked out of a rehab facility. I laughed with her, but I considered the debacle to be no laughing matter.

My mom was transferred to a facility in Athens. That was a much better situation for me because my school and apartment were there, and I needed to take my exams. Everything was progressing, and then my mom developed a fever. They suspended her treatment again. The law school had agreed to postpone my exams, but the dean was getting impatient. He was concerned that the passage of time would hinder my ability to complete them. We had already scheduled several dates that I was unable to keep.

I called one of my life-long friends, and he agreed to

come to the hospital. We prayed for my mom's fever to break. We went into her room, and he asked my mom a pointed question, "Do you want to live or have you given up?" She said, "No. I want to live!"

That's all we needed to hear. If she maintained her resolve to fight, we would join her. I closed the doors to her room, and we entered intense spiritual warfare. I employed every strategy I'd learned from the past few years of tragedy. I had lost so many of the people I loved; I wasn't giving my mom up without a fight. We spent hours, praying, declaring victory, and singing. Finally after hours of warfare, the fever broke! We dance and sang around the room. We thanked God for giving us the victory. I left the room and went home to get a few hours of sleep. I would have to study for my exam. The first was scheduled in two days!

The following morning, I opted to take the later shift for sitting with my mom. My brother went to be with her during the morning. After getting a couple of hours of extra sleep, I gathered my books and notes to study. I was quizzing myself when my cell phone rang. I answered it and heard my mom on the other line. I asked her how the morning went and whether they had started the treatment. At that point, she told me to hold the line. She said someone needed to talk with me.

The woman who came on the line introduced herself as the palliative care nurse. I had no idea what that meant, so I allowed her to continue. She took a breath and said, "Ms. Mayfield, there is nothing else we can do for your mother. We are sending her home under hospice care." Wait? What did she just say? Had we not prayed and interceded all night? Hadn't my mom's fever broken? Why weren't they starting the cancer treatment as planned? My heart started beating really fast, and I swallowed hard. Suddenly, I blurted the barrage of questions that had just played out in my head. She told me that there was no need to initiate treatment because the cancer was spreading. More importantly, the lung procedure she had made it impossible to treat the areas of the lung that were metastasizing most aggressively. I could not bear the news she delivered. I wanted my dad. I couldn't breathe.

My mom took the phone and began speaking, "Adrienne, it is okay. They have decided that there is nothing they can do. They are sending me home to die. I need you to come up to the hospital now and complete the paperwork. They need you to sign some forms. One of them is my request not to be resuscitated. Can you come now so we can begin the release process?"

She was so calm. Too calm. She was matter-of-fact in her demand of me. Though she was dying, her authority had long been firmly established. I said, "But?" She quickly dismissed me. "No, Adrienne. Come to the hospital now. I need you to do that." I mumbled, "OK," and hung up the phone. What would I do now? My first exam was in the morning. I had already requested that they be rescheduled twice. The hospital was releasing my mom. They said she was dying. My entire world was falling apart.

I hurriedly threw on some clothes and washed the tears from my face. If nothing else, I wanted my mom to see my strength. I had to be there for her. I couldn't let her see me falling apart. I sat down at my laptop and quickly typed an email to the Dean. I told him about the call I had just received and noted that I was heading to the hospital to finalize the paperwork. I asked for one last extension to Wednesday (It was Friday at the time) so I could have time to get my mother released and settled in at home. I gave him my word that should he agree, I would take my exam on Wednesday, no matter what.

When I arrived at the hospital, the palliative care nurse

was waiting in the room. I could tell by her face that she was bracing for a confrontation, but I was still in shock. She began talking. Most of what she said was just background noise for me. I was focused on my mom's face. I went to her and grabbed her hand. She looked up and smiled. The nurse had a stack of papers for me to sign as the power of attorney. I skimmed every line, methodically, like I'd been trained to do in law school, and signed my name. Signing the "Do Not Resuscitate" form was like signing my mom's life away. Many families argue and fight over who will make end of life decisions, but trust me: you do not really want to be the one to do it. No one does.

The nurse whisked the forms away and I went back into my mom's room. She tried to explain what had transpired since I left the hospital, but none of it made sense. They had told us that if the fever broke, they would start the radiation treatment again. We prayed, and the fever broke; now they were saying my mom was being sent home to die. We sat in the room for a few hours waiting for them to process the paperwork, and then we took Mom home.

I was scared to check my email, but I needed to know the Dean's response. When I checked, there was no email. There was no way I would be able to take my exam. I had not studied. At all. I decided to call his office. My heart was beating so loudly; I could hear it in my head. I had no time to prepare. I had too much on my plate. If he said no, I would likely fail. He answered the phone and apologized for forgetting to respond. Thankfully, he agreed to my request. I was so grateful. His decision gave me the freedom to spend the weekend getting my mom settled and dealing with her diagnosis.

That Sunday, one of the local pastors called to ask if he could bring communion to my mom. She wanted to take it, so I agreed. I knew him from our old church. He came over with one of the ministers and administered the sacraments. Afterwards, he gave me his number, asked if we needed anything, and told me that he would be praying for us.

The doctors had given us little hope, so we tried to make the most of the time with my mom. I monitored the food she was given very closely. I was very strict about sugar since I knew that sugar feeds cancers cells. Something very peculiar happened. My mom actually started getting better. We charted her vitals every day and they actually began to improve. The hospice nurse told us not to give up hope. She was a Christian, so she joined us in praying for a miracle.

My mom had retired from the city council the previous December. One of the projects she had worked on was a new city hall. Just as she was released from the hospital, the project was completed. One day my brother and I asked her if she wanted to go to take a look. She was hesitant; she thought loading her and the portable oxygen machine would be too much of a hassle. We assured her that she wasn't a burden. She was so happy and excited. We drove her around town and circled around the new city hall. She was thrilled with how it turned out.

We also had a surprise for her. We drove to her sister's house in the country. When we pulled up outside, my aunt screamed in delight. I will never forget that day. My mom was so happy to be out doing something normal. We drove back home and for the first time in a long time, I felt a sense of peace envelope me.

After my mom had been home for about three weeks, I went home to my apartment for a day. The next day, when I returned, she was markedly worse. She seemed weak and feeble, and she was hallucinating. My aunts came to sit with her that night, and we were all perplexed by the decline. I later discovered that someone had given her four times the dosage of morphine we had been instructed to give her. She was incoherent and lethargic, and she spoke of things that were long past. Not knowing what else to do, I called the communion pastor to come to pray. He came and prayed for her.

She made it through the night, but it was clear that she was deteriorating. While I was preparing her lunch, one of her friends tried to help my mom shift in the chair. The friend lost her footing and my mom fell on the floor. I ran into the den when I heard the loud thud. My mom couldn't lift herself into the chair, and she was too heavy for us. My brother came to help, but she was still too heavy. Her body was like dead weight. I ran to the door to get help. Thankfully my cousin was outside. He ran up the hill and came inside. He and my brother lifted my mom back into the chair like a little baby. As I watched this whole chain of events, I could feel my mom slipping away. She had always been fiercely independent. When I looked into her eyes, I could see that her spirit was broken. She did not want to live like that.

Later that afternoon, I decided to take a shower. While I was in the bathroom, my siblings called 911. My brother knocked on the bathroom door and told me that they were taking her. I was fuming! We all knew that Mom was sent home by the hospital under hospice care. Taking her back would serve no point. They had already told us they planned no further treatment. By the time I came out of the shower, I saw the ambulance going up the road with Mom.

I put on my clothes and waited. About thirty minutes later, I got the call. It was my sister. "Adrienne, we need you to come to the hospital to sign the papers for mom's admittance. They won't let us admit her without you." I wanted to scream at her and tell her I knew that, but I couldn't subject Mom to any more indecision and chaos.

I jumped in my car and made the drive to Anderson, S.C., about 26 miles away. I was in shock. I should not have been driving. When I arrived, I asked to be taken to my mom. She appeared comfortable, but she had a huge CPAP covering her face. Her eyes had begun to have a grayish film over them, and her breathing was labored. I told her how much I loved her and tried to assure her that everything was going to be fine. A frog was welling in my throat. This was too much. Though I tried to think positively, deep down, I knew this was the beginning of the end.

After about ten minutes, the nurse came to get me for a consult with the doctor. I felt so stupid talking to him. I explained that though we already knew my mom's condition, my siblings had called the ambulance because they didn't know what else to do. He seemed relieved that he wasn't going to have to give me the bad news. I asked if he would talk to them. He agreed and brought them in. The doctor gave us two alternatives; we could take her back home or she could be transferred to the hospital's hospice care floor. I told him we were taking her home; he agreed to take care of all the arrangements.

I went back to my mother's room and told her we were taking her home. She nodded her head. I grabbed my phone and played two of her favorite songs, "Nobody Greater" by Vashawn Mitchell and "Let the Church Say Amen" by Marvin Winans. She tried to sing along, so I did too. Ironically there was a mother and daughter sitting in the nearby emergency room bed. The mother came over to me with tears in her eyes and said, "This is a great thing you are doing here for your mom. I can see that she is very sick. God bless you." I nodded in appreciation and kept singing along. I lay on my mom's chest and said, "I love you so much, Ma." She smiled at me and said, "I love you too." The EMTs were coming to transport her home. They loaded her into the ambulance and I took the long walk to my car—one of the longest walks I have ever taken.

My brother and sister went ahead so they could meet the EMTs when they arrived. When I got home, my mom wasn't conscious anymore. Her breathing was slow and she didn't open her eyes. I went into the kitchen to finish my salad. When I finished, I went to check on her. I wanted to check her oxygen level, so I grabbed the pulse oximeter. Her level was under 40%! I began screaming at the family members who were seated in the room. "She's barely breathing! What are you doing? Get up! Do something!" My brother ran to the garage and pushed the oxygen level higher, but nothing changed. Finally, my sister came over and closed my mom's mouth. It fell open again. My brother tested her oxygen level again, and it had fallen to into the 20s. He looked back at everyone and said, "She's leaving." Within seconds the machine changed to zero. We took it out to reset it, but the number still showed zero. I stood beside my mother, looked down at her and said, "So this is how you're going? Like this? You didn't even say goodbye." A tear rolled down my face. One of my cousins shrieked loudly and ran into the kitchen. She hid underneath the table.

It all felt like a dream. I calmly walked over to the phone and called 911. I told them that my mother had died so they would need to call the coroner. When the ambulance arrived, the EMT dragged my mom's limp body to the floor. It made a loud thud. I wanted to kick the EMT for doing that, but I just stood there. I knew she was already gone, so I suppose it really didn't matter.

My hometown is small. Many people live by their police scanners, so news was already spreading. People started piling into the house, standing around my mom's lifeless body. I could not believe their insensitivity, but I was too numb to address it. The EMT checked for a pulse then looked around and asked, "Who's in charge here?" I stepped forward and he pulled me into the back room. He basically told me that my mom was gone. He said they could resuscitate her and keep her alive. His exact words were, "We can hook a piece of meat to a machine and keep it alive, but that's not what you want." I asked him if there was any pulse. He told me there wasn't. I mumbled, "Just let her go."

I walked back into the den and looked at all the people standing around gawking at my mom's body. I asked them all to leave and give us some privacy. I grabbed my sister and brother's hands and said, "Let's sing. The angels are ushering Ma into heaven. We have to celebrate."

It was almost as if I could sense what was transpiring in the spirit realm even though the natural scene had not changed. We fumbled over a chorus or two and everyone began crying. I went to the phone and called the mortician and asked him to come. Then, I called her pastor and told him we needed to schedule her funeral.

Two months after my mother's diagnosis, she was gone. Two short months. There were many details to address—obituary verbiage, picture choices, outfits, caskets, funeral participants, etc. By now, I was becoming skilled at handling these affairs. Too skilled. My siblings and I tried to work together, but the tension of grief and loss began to take its toll. Rather than coming together as my mother had prayed, a wedge of separation began forming between us. Thankfully, we were able to get everything sorted and my mother was laid to rest four days later. The local pastor who had come to pray for her agreed to do a part of the service, and he came by the house to make sure we were okay. His niceties were appreciated because I needed a friend.

4. PAIN AS A MATCHMAKER
WHAT IS THE DANGER OF MAKING MAJOR DECISIONS WHEN YOU ARE NOT WHOLE?

There were many tasks to complete at my mom's house so I stayed there. She had papers and files from the 70's! I knew it would take the remainder of my summer to get everything in line. The communion pastor's church was down the street, so I decided to go there on Sundays. I knew better than to skip church during this period in my life. I was confident that God was the only reason I had not lost my mind.

After I went there a couple of Sundays, he approached me after church. He asked how things were going and said, "Would it be okay for me to call you?" I wondered why he was asking me that since he had texted a few times over the past weeks. When I looked up, he smiled sheepishly. Then it dawned on me. Oh! He wanted to CALL me. Then I understood. I agreed that it would be fine and walked away.

He called that night and we chatted. It felt weird. I couldn't help wondering if pastors should call women. Was it appropriate? To make matters even more complicated, he and his family had been members of my family's former church. He was a widower. His wife had died tragically a couple of years before. I knew his former wife and his children. In fact, I had been his son's principal at the middle school.

I thought maybe we could just be friends and support each other through our grief. My apprehension and

49

unanswered questions should have signaled the "press pause button," but they didn't. We continued to converse and went out on a few dates. We were careful to be very discreet. I was very concerned how a dating pastor might appear to everyone.

I spent the next couple of months cleaning and organizing my parent's house. I barely had time to breathe before it was time for my second year of law school to begin. I strongly considered requesting a deferment, but I knew myself all too well. Had I taken a year off, I likely would not have ever returned. Besides, I felt it was my duty to continue. God had given me the strength to complete my first year of law school while burying my mom. He even kept me from failing my exams! I decided that the return to something normal might actually be good for me.

The pastor and I were seeing each other regularly, and he had no appreciation for the rigor of my school program. He was an Army veteran who had enlisted right after high school. He met his wife a few weeks later and they married. They remain married for 20 years until she passed away. Our life paths had been very different. I was highly educated, and I had dated liberally.

He demanded to see me every weekend. That left me little time to organize myself, handle my mom's affairs, and study. At first, I found his preoccupation with my every move charming. In short order, it became suffocating.

He was a bi-vocational pastor who worked third shift. He always wanted to talk before he went to sleep, then he'd want to call later, around midnight, for "prayer." I wasn't always available, and when I wasn't, he would be very irritated. His irritation would lead to a barrage of questions about my whereabouts—where I'd been, who I had been with, why I missed his call.

I knew there was something off about his behavior, but I was very broken. My family was estranged due to some of my mom's affairs, so I had no one else. Grief is a very powerful motivator. It makes people do things they otherwise would not do. It also hinders the ability to make rational and logical decisions. When grief is coupled with the pain that naturally comes with great loss, one can easily become functionally dysfunctional. Such was the case with me. I continued with my life and responsibilities as if I had not just been through very significant traumas. To continue to "function" as normal when life is anything but that is clearly dysfunctional.

We continued to date but we did not tell anyone. We decided that we would announce our relationship by attending my family Christmas party together. When we walked in together that December, all the air left the room. Everyone was in shock! I knew I'd have a lot of questions to answer. We "went public" at church in much the same way. I'd already been attending regularly, so most of the church members probably already knew.

Meanwhile law school was intensifying. My classmates were getting job offers for the summer. Many were returning to the same firms they had worked for the previous summer. Because I had spent my summer caring for my mom, I didn't have any strong leads. I decided that my best option would be to take a couple of summer courses so I could lighten my load for my last year.

One night, I missed my boyfriend's call. I kept trying to call him back, but he wouldn't answer. I decided it was probably best since I needed to complete some homework anyway. About an hour later, I was watching television and eating dinner. I heard a tap on my door. I hesitated because I wasn't expecting anyone. I tiptoed to the door and looked through the peephole. It was him! I opened the door. I was very surprised because he should have been at work. He pushed past me, blurting, "What are you doing?" I looked around dumbfounded. When I asked about work, he told me he called in because he couldn't stop worrying about me. His behavior was starting to make me feel uncomfortable, but I didn't know how to stop it. I told him to have a seat and offered him a cup of coffee.

It should be noted that he claimed to have a very strong prophetic gift. Often he would tell me that God was showing him things about our relationship and how we were supposed to be together. Though I had a very intimate relationship of my own with God by then, I allowed my boyfriend's "experiences" and "visions" to influence my thinking. I should have known better than to trust someone else's interpretation of God's plans for me, but I wasn't thinking clearly.

The previous ten years of my life had been fraught with extreme difficulty and loss. I had buried my grandparents, my father, and my mother, and I also had shepherded my brother through a near death experience. The trauma and stress had taken a tremendous toll. Besides, my mother was the person I would normally have sought for wisdom on this issue, and she was gone. For more than a short while, I just allowed myself to wander aimlessly in the dark.

There was also a significant issue brewing with my only remaining grandparent. My grandfather remarried when he was 83. A few years after his marriage, he started forgetting things and becoming more aggressive. After many doctor's visits, he was diagnosed with dementia. His new wife tried for a while to take care of him, but it became too much. Finally, she decided to place him in a nursing home.

I went to see him a few times. He talked to me, and he seemed to know who I was, but he was very frail and thin. My great-grandfather had lived to be 96, and my grandfather was 93. He was the last man standing. I only had one grandparent left.

My grandfather served in the army and taught himself to draft blueprints and build houses with only a fifth grade education. He actually built our house and most of the houses in my neighborhood. He had three daughters. There was no son to train, so he taught my mom everything he knew since she was the oldest. He was a very smart man, but he was also miserly. I remember having to beg him for .15 to buy a Popsicle when I was a kid. Perhaps that was part of his personality. He was an astute businessman.

I drove home to see him one weekend. He was very quiet for most of the visit. His condition was deteriorating. Dementia is a very cruel disease. It transforms an adult into a helpless child. It was extremely painful to look at my grandfather in that state. That following week, I received a call that my grandfather had passed away.

By this time, none of my family was speaking to me. Some said they were angry with the amount of control I exerted over my mom's care, visitation schedule, funeral planning, etc. Most sided with my sister and brother in what they viewed as an unequal "balance of power."

Whatever their reasons, I lived in isolation. I did not have a family anymore. I couldn't take the drama and tension, so I skipped the funeral altogether.

I was alienated from my siblings, and I didn't have anyone else. My boyfriend was very observant; he began to isolate me. If I had to collaborate or interact with a male classmate, he was very angry. He called me names and told me that I was flirting with them. On more than one occasion, he told me that he hoped I wouldn't become a lawyer. He accused me of being prideful and arrogant, and said God was not going to let it continue. Everything about me that I considered an asset became a target for his insults and aggression.

I had always been self-confident and independent, but that was all changing. It is worth mentioning again that I am 6'0 tall. I am no shrinking violet. I had always been very outspoken and self-assured. My reputation had always been one of dignity, self-respect and class. My boyfriend was much shorter than me. I often wondered if there was a Napoleon complex at work. Maybe the verbal abuse was his attempt to equalize us.

I was slowly becoming a shell of myself. Even though his accusations were not true, I found myself often wondering if they were. I began to second guess every decision I made. Around September of that year, we went to Augusta, GA. He had planned a few days away, so I agreed. We went to visit my cousin first and then headed to one of my favorite restaurants. As I finished up my food, I went to the bathroom. When I returned, I sat down to eat my last few bites. He slid from his seat and got down on one knee. He pulled out a ring and asked me to marry him!

A proposal is on the top of the list for most 30-something year old women, and I was no different. I had always hoped to be married and have six children. I envisioned the American dream. After all, I'd worked for it! Still, I needed to consider the past year dating this man. He was becoming increasingly more jealous and controlling. He dictated every aspect of my life and influenced my behavior by his acceptance or rejection of me. On top of all that, I had just buried my mother, and I was in law school.

In less than ten months, I would be sitting for the Georgia bar. I needed to focus on the responsibilities that lay ahead. I didn't need the distraction of being engaged, planning a wedding, trying to help pastor a church, and parenting two adult step-children. I subconsciously knew these all these things, but my ability to process my decisions was stifled by pain.

Pain is a terrible lens through which to make decisions, but I didn't realize it then. I was so used to pretending to "be okay" that I didn't realize I was broken. I got caught in the emotion of the moment and said, "Yes!" I immediately called my brother and my best friend. They were as shocked as I was.

Just as I should have been trying to prepare for the Georgia bar and land a great job, I allowed myself to be manipulated into another life. I had just spent the last ten years of my life taking care of others, basically putting my own life on hold and making sacrifices for them. I was actually looking forward to making decisions without considering anyone else. My affirmative answer ensured that my wish would not come true. Wedding and shower planning began almost immediately. Although I was able to get him to agree to a yearlong engagement, I still didn't have much time.

Even my professors at school were skeptical of my decision. I remember going to meet with one of my favorite professors. I told him I had gotten engaged. I expected him to be happy, but he was not. He looked me squarely in the eye and asked, "Ms. Mayfield, are you sure this is something you should be doing right now? You just lost your mom. You are trying to finish law school. You have to be serious if you want to pass the bar. Can this wait?" I smiled and told him I was waiting a year for the actual wedding.

They say hindsight is 20/20. Apparently it is true. Even as I compile my narrative, I am beginning to see small warnings that came on more than one occasion. Sadly, I was too blind to take heed to their wisdom.

About six months later, my fiancé and I went out to dinner. We were casually talking when he asked me about a former boyfriend—one I had dated no less than 15 year prior. He wanted to know if I had spoken with him. I had nothing to hide. We had spoken when I got engaged, so I told the truth. As soon as I released the words, I knew I'd made a huge mistake. His face turned red. He angrily motioned for the waitress. When she came to the table, he screamed, "Cancel the food. We're leaving!" I didn't know what to do except to follow him out the door.

When we reached the car, he became even more enraged. "Who do you think I am? I am not marrying a whore. I am not going to take this! I won't!" Something in my gut told me silence was golden, so I didn't respond. When he arrived at my apartment, he put me out and kept going. I walked inside and sat speechless on the couch.

I was in trouble, and I knew it. The question was how I was I going to get out. The timing of things was more than ironic. I had just begun a semester of internship at my law school's family violence clinic. On a daily basis, I listened to stories of women who were in similar situations. Although their situations seemed much more dangerous, their narratives had all begun much like the nightmare I was living in. So I knew the signs. I knew I needed to get away from him. His behavior that night was yet another warning.

After an hour or so, he returned to the apartment with a paper bag. I shouldn't have let him in, but I was too afraid. Who could I tell? No one would believe that I, Adrienne "everything is going for her" Mayfield was allowing myself to be treated this way. Even I had great difficulty accepting that this was my life.

He went upstairs and slammed the door in the guest bedroom. I sat downstairs quietly not really knowing what to do. Finally, a thought from my former self popped into my head. "What are you doing sitting here like a little child? This is your apartment! March up those stairs and tell him to get out of your house. Make him go home. You don't have to deal with this!"

Suddenly, I felt empowered and I marched upstairs. I threw the door open and walked in. There, in the corner on the floor, sat my fiancé with a 40 oz. by his side. I knew this was not going to end well. He had been an alcoholic in the military and had only given up alcohol a few years before when he accepted Christ. I looked at him and asked him what he was doing. He started calling random people and saying terrible things to them on the phone.

Then he started taunting me, "Satan is standing behind you, and he's laughing. He's laughing at you. You're so stupid!" I became upset. I screamed, "No he's laughing at you. Look at you, you're drunk. Get out! Get out of my house, now!" He staggered up and pushed past me. He went into my bedroom and locked the door. Now what was I going to do? This was a nightmare! Where was my mom when I needed her? Where was my dad?

I went downstairs and tried to calm down. A short time later, he opened the door and asked me to come upstairs. When I walked into the room, he told me he had taken some pills. He said he didn't want to live. Fear overtook me. I ran downstairs to grab my cell phone and called 911. The EMTs arrived shortly and I told them what happened. They went upstairs to talk to him. In his drunken stupor he began crying, telling them I was cheating on him and how we were supposed to be getting married. They listened and took copious notes. I tried to head upstairs, but one of them stopped me. "Ma'am, it will be best if you stay downstairs while we complete the evaluation. I'm asking you to stay downstairs." Here, he was telling me I couldn't go upstairs in my own apartment all because of him! I was done.

I waited patiently for them to take him away. After about 45 minutes, the EMTs headed down the stairwell. Wait! Why weren't they taking HIM? The EMT looked at me sadly, "Ma'am, he has refused to go with us, and we can't take him without his consent. He took quite a few Tylenol. That coupled with the alcohol will knock him out for a while, but he'll be okay. He just needs to sleep it off." I interrupted him. "So you're not taking him? What am I supposed to do with him? He doesn't live here!" They continued to walk down the stairs. The EMT looked back at me and said, "I'm sorry. There's nothing else we can do. He has refused treatment." With that, they walked out the door, leaving me alone with him.

I wish I could say I ended the relationship, but I did not. I was too embarrassed to tell anyone, and after that encounter with him, I knew he was unstable. I also knew he would not just let me walk away from him. I felt weak and powerless. Not only did I stay in the relationship, but I also moved forward with our wedding plans.

I continued with school and graduated a few months later. I began the process of preparing for the bar, but I was too preoccupied. I was traveling home twice a week for church services, handling my mom's estate, and trying to study. Every weekend, my fiancé demanded that he see me. No exceptions. This was a recipe for disaster, and I knew it.

At times, I wondered if he was purposefully trying to sabotage my efforts. He had, on more than one occasion, expressed his disinterest in my becoming a lawyer—even though he knew those were my aspirations when we met. Needless to say, my bar results were not favorable. I did not pass. I was very disappointed, but not surprised. The bar is a high stakes test. I had not had the opportunity to properly prepare. I was too distracted.

We started pre-marital counseling and it was not going well either. One day we were driving to get something to eat. He stopped at a red light and gazed over in my direction. He said, "You know when we get married, if you ever cheat on me I will kill you?" Whoa! I just looked down. Finally, I got up the nerve to ask, "What did you just say to me?" He said, "I mean it. I couldn't take it." Since he repeated it, I knew there was nothing else for me to say. I remained silent for the rest of the trip.

That week, I shared his words with our marriage counselor. They asked him if he had said that, and he admitted it. That was basically the end of the session. They told us the wedding needed to be called off. They would not support us going forward. I was relieved. Finally someone else was saying what I had lost the courage to say.

That following week, his pastor's pastor called. He wanted to talk with him about the session. The counselors had told him what I shared. He told my fiancé that the wedding needed to be postponed so he could get some help. I listened intently for his response. My fiancé told him we were fine. After he hung up the phone, he told me we would find another counselor. He said he didn't like them anyway because they only talked about themselves.

All this drama happened while I was studying to take the bar exam again. I poured myself into my studies and tried to pretend I wasn't living my reality. There were many days where I just filled my practice sheets with my tears. I could not believe this was my life. Still, I moved forward with my wedding plans. I knew I was making a huge mistake, but I had no idea how to get away from him. I needed to stabilize something because it seemed my life was reeling out of control.

I had spent my entire life on top of my game. My whole existence had been marked by successes. Everything I attempted, I achieved. Now that had all changed. The emotional abuse broke my spirit. My weakened self-esteem also suffered a tremendous blow when I failed the exam. My life was beginning to take on a different tenor that I did not like.

5. ELEPHANT IN THE ROOM

WHAT HAPPENS WHEN YOU ARE TOO DISTRACTED TO HEAR GOD'S VOICE?

The week of the wedding I decided to surprise my fiancé by taking him to lunch while I was in town. I called him on my way but I gave no indication I was headed there. He seemed a little distracted, but I paid it no attention. I dropped by the florist to finalize details and headed to his house. I pulled up quietly and walked around the back of the house. His truck was home. I tapped on the door and waited and waited and waited. Finally he came to the door. He looked surprised, but not pleasantly so. He asked, "What are you doing here?" Although he tried to muster a smile, the tension in his body was undeniable. When I hugged him, I could sense that something was very wrong.

I walked past him and took a seat on his bed. He said he was about to shower, so I got his phone. I decided to call to book the officiant's hotel while I waited. I picked up his phone and clicked on Safari. A pornographic image and video started to play! I threw the phone down. I couldn't believe what I was seeing. Who were these naked people? It was four days before my wedding! I picked the phone up again to make sure I hadn't accidentally pressed something. The image was still there.

My heart felt like it was pumping out of my chest. My throat was dry. Tears were forming in my eyes. There . . . was . . . pornography. . . on . . . MY . .fiancé's . . .phone!

I took several deep breaths and placed the phone face

down. I waited for what seemed like hours for him to finish his shower and get dressed. He seemed much calmer as he asked, "So where you wanna eat, babe?" I asked him to sit down, and I handed him the phone. He was so calm; it was scary. He tried to explain it away by saying he hadn't even looked at it. He was just checking out some things on the web to get ready for the honeymoon since he was very nervous. Each word that came out of his mouth was a lie, and I knew it. He had been married for 20 years. He was no virgin. He didn't need pointers from a pornography video to make him comfortable having sex. Who was he kidding? I told him I didn't believe him. I gathered my keys, and I walked out. All the way home, my hands were shaking. What was I going to do? I needed someone to help me.

I called an older woman I knew and asked for her advice. She said, "Adrienne, God loves you. He has shown you the truth about the man you plan to marry. The question now is what are you going to do? Are you going to go forward with this wedding or not? It is your choice but you will not go in blindly. God has shown you the heart of the man you're marrying." Everything she said was true but my heart was not prepared to hear it. I was trying to convince myself that he was not addicted to pornography.

There had to be some mistake. This could not be happening. I kept telling myself maybe this was his first time. I knew the things he told me were lies, but I almost wanted to believe them. If he was, in fact, a porn addict, I couldn't marry him. He needed help. Besides, what else was he hiding from me? There was too much deception to move forward.

So I did what people do when they are uncomfortable with the first opinion. I went for a second one! I called one of my friends and her husband for advice. Her husband wanted to talk to him. Surprisingly, my fiancé agreed. My friend's husband pressed him for truth, but he was not honest. He continued with the lie about watching to prepare for the wedding night. They prayed for us and told us that we should take communion together. They instructed him to decree the scripture from Psalms about not looking on any unclean thing. My fiancé also promised that if the issue ever came up again, I could walk away. Just typing those words sounds ridiculous enough. It's hard to believe I moved forward with a lifelong covenant under these terms, but I did.

The wedding ceremony was beautiful. It really is hard to believe. Despite our mistakes and bad decisions, God is gracious. He allowed me to have a beautiful wedding. It was the wedding of my dreams.

We went to Jamaica for our honeymoon and actually had a pretty good time. The honeymoon night, however, was awkward. I could tell that it was not only because we had waited to sleep together. There was a feeling like he wished I was someone else. I'm not sure if the feeling was real or maybe it was a subconscious reaction from my discovery. Either way, I just knew something didn't feel right.

The bliss and newness of marriage was very short-lived. About a month into the marriage, we were lying in bed. He wanted me to Google something with his phone, so he handed it to me. Instead of going to Google, I went to his Internet history. There were 13 different porn sites listed. I handed the phone to him. He simply retorted, "Well, what are you going to do? You can't help me." That was his response. I crawled out of bed and went downstairs.

The next month I traveled to Atlanta to one of my friend's swearing-in ceremony. Afterwards, her father took us out to eat. I decided to drop by a visit my best friend since I hadn't seen her since the wedding. I figured it would be okay since my husband would be sleeping before he went to work. Boy was I wrong! He called me right after I got there and demanded that I come home. It was already 7:00. It would take me a little over an hour to get home, and he would leave for work at 9:30. I told him I wanted to visit her for a little while. He hung up the phone.

In about twenty minutes, he called me back and said he wasn't going to work. Instead, he was going to meet his friend to get a gun. He began ranting about not being stupid, knowing that I was cheating on him, and that I could have that man if I wanted him. I had no idea what he was talking about but hearing conversation about a gun reminded me of what he had told me at the stop light.

I told him he needed to calm down and go to work as planned. I honestly thought he was attention seeking, so I called his friend who sold guns. He confirmed that they were supposed to be meeting at 10:00. He was going to sell him a gun! I decided that there was no way I could go home. I had to stay at my friend's house. I called another one of his friends, told him what transpired, and asked him to go to our house. I had absolutely no experience with this type of behavior. I did not know what else to do.

His friend went to the apartment and was able to get him settled down. He stayed with him through the night and told me he would call me. I was afraid to go home, but I knew I could not stay gone forever. Besides, I knew the longer I stayed away, the madder he'd be.

I returned home the next day, not really sure what I'd find.

Fortunately, he was calm and very apologetic. A few weeks of serenity followed, and then we went out to dinner one weekend. When we came home, we went upstairs. I stayed downstairs to watch television. As I sat there, I saw a light coming from the corner of the couch. I looked over to see where it was coming from. There was a tablet stuffed behind the cypress tree! It wasn't mine. I didn't even know he had another device!

I didn't want to look at it, but I needed to know the truth. I turned it on and clicked on the Internet. Twenty-six pornographic websites were listed on the screen! I placed it back where I found it and went upstairs to bed. I couldn't process all of this. I needed to rest. We hadn't even been married three months.

At this point, many of you are likely shocked about these revelations. I, too, had no idea that pornography use was such a pervasive issue in the church. However, according to a survey by the Barna Group in 2014, 64% who men who self-identified as Christians and 15% of women viewed pornography at least once a month. Thirty-seven percent of Christian men and 7% of Christian women viewed pornography at least several times a week. These numbers are quite troubling and we must do something to address this growing epidemic.

Although accessing pornography is easier than it has ever been, the stigma attached to its use forces users into a life of secrecy and deception. Such was the case with my husband. He knew that using pornography was wrong. He was fully aware of the Bible's teachings concerning lust. So he tried to hide his addiction from everyone, including me. However, I could no longer hide my head in the sand. This new discovery pushed me to stop living in denial—I was married to an addict.

I couldn't take it anymore. I asked him to leave. Another couple was walking through the saga with us, and they told him it was the only fair thing to do. They encouraged him to leave so we could fast and pray. He was extremely hesitant, but he finally agreed to go. He also gave me his keys to the apartment.

He was only gone for one night before he started calling and texting my phone non-stop. He kept saying how much he loved me and that he couldn't be at home alone. He begged me to let him come home. When I reminded him that the separation was a time for us to fast and pray, he hung up the phone.

The next morning, around 6:00 a.m., I heard a knock on the door. I tiptoed downstairs only to discover that it was him. I tiptoed back up the stairs and went into the restroom. In a matter of seconds, I heard a loud crashing sound. Fear tore through my entire being. What was happening? Was I going to die? I ran downstairs to see what was going on. As I turned the corner, I saw him. He had come through the kitchen window!

The look of terror in his eyes told me I needed to stay calm. I walked forward slowly and tried not to excite him. He ran to me, like a small child, and began hugging me. "I can't. I won't live without you. I need you." I was scared but not stupid. I knew making him angry would be a big mistake. I led him to the couch and tried to talk softly. "Honey, you have to leave. You can't be here. We're supposed to be praying. You have to give me some time to process all of this." He didn't like my response. He started to get agitated and said he would not leave. This was our home, he argued. Just as he was talking, I got a text the woman who was counseling us with her husband. She was checking in. I simply texted back "He's here!" She began calling my phone, but he wouldn't let me answer. Then her husband began calling him. He wouldn't take his call either. I urged him to pick up the phone, reminding him that we didn't want them to worry. Finally he picked up the phone and the pastor was able to convince him to leave.

At that point, I felt like legal intervention was inevitable. I knew I needed to get a restraining order, but he had proven that it would take more than a piece of paper to keep him away from me. I was far too acquainted with the stories of women whose abusers violated their TPO's and came after them. I just never thought I would be one of them.

The women and their children lived through experiences that were filled with trauma, pain, and unspeakable fear. As I assisted my clients, I was able to gain a new perspective on a question many people ask, "Why does she stay? Why doesn't she just leave?" I'd always wondered myself, and I shamelessly admit that I had always judged the victims as weak or stupid. I no longer viewed them that way. Every day I lived with unimaginable fear. Now that I had switched places with my clients, I finally understood.

The next day he pretended to need something from the house. I knew I could never live like this. If he was not going to let me have any peace, I figured I might as well let him come home. At least then I wouldn't sit up in my bed at night wondering if he was breaking in. He was grateful that I let him come home, so things were better for a while.

I was prepping to take the bar again, so he promised to let me study. The tranquility was short-lived. One night, as we slept in bed, my husband began talking about how unloved he felt. I turned toward him and braced for what might happen next. All of a sudden, he took both of his hands, wrapped them around his throat and started choking himself! His face started contorting and his voice deepened, "I told you I was going to kill you. I mean, I told you I was going to kill him!" I immediately sat up in my bed and started praying out loud. I grabbed his hands and peeled them from his throat. He took a few deep breaths and grabbed his throat again. I prayed more fervently this time, commanding everything evil to vacate our bedroom in Jesus' name.

Finally, I felt a sense of calm fill the room as he started

to cry. That was a pivotal moment for me. I was forced to accept the reality of my situation. This was no fairy tale. I was not a blissful newlywed. I was in a battle for my life!

Life was extremely awkward for a few days. Finally I found the nerve to ask him about the incident. When I asked him what happened, he said he didn't remember the event. I mentioned it in our counseling session, but nothing was ever resolved. He continued to maintain that everything was fine. Things were far from fine, but sadly the dysfunction was starting to feel normal.

One day we sat in the den watching television. A former male co-worker called to ask some questions about taking the LSAT. Even though I held the conversation right in from of my husband, he was furious. As soon as I hung up the phone, he began ranting. He said I disrespected him by taking the call. "No respectable married woman would be taking calls from men," he screamed. "What else are you hiding?" he wondered aloud. He grabbed my phone and started going through my call log. Though nothing was there, he was not satisfied. He headed for my laptop and started going through the pictures, deleting some of them. No male picture was acceptable, even graduation pictures with some of my students were targets. He deleted them all! Christmas parties with my brother and his friends were also deleted. In his rage, he even inadvertently deleted some of the files I was using to study for the bar, and I was retaking the test in four days!

After he was finished, he stormed upstairs and closed the door. When he got ready for church the next morning, I told him I wasn't going. While he was gone, I packed my things, drove to Atlanta, and checked into a hotel. I could not allow this saga to destroy my test results again. I had to focus.

The night before the exam, the hotel phone rang. The

ringer scared me because no one knew the hotel I had chosen. I picked up the phone, and said, "Hello?" It was him! I assume he remembered that we stayed at that hotel for our honeymoon. It was near the test site. Something an abuse victim learns too late is the skill of only revealing as much information as necessary. This is a very difficult skill to master because a marriage is the most intimate relationship.

Trying to remember to withhold behavior patterns and locations can be difficult to manage, but it is a skill necessary for safety. When I was preparing for my honeymoon, I had no reason to withhold my hotel information. I had no reason not to point out the location of the test site. Those pieces of information were now being used against me. He had tracked me down. I asked him why he was calling me. He pretended to be concerned and said he wanted to wish me well on the test. Naturally, I found his sincerity questionable.

I took the exam both days and decided to go to my brother's house for a few days. I needed to formulate a plan of action, and I couldn't go home to do it. He called my phone incessantly. He demanded to know where I was. He continually reminded me that I was his wife. I did not budge. When I decided that it would be best not to take his calls, he switched his efforts to my brother.

One of the conditions of staying together had been the installation of monitoring software for his phone. The program monitored his Internet usage and sent a weekly report. I decided it would be a good time to review the weekly report as I planned my next move. I opened my email and searched for the report. It was marked in all red for high alert. He had spent most of the week on Facebook pages of women we knew, but he upped the ante a bit. There were inquiries from Backpages, Google searches for massage parlors, and he had even Googled "how to ask your massage therapist an embarrassing question!"

I could not believe what I was reading. He knew that I would get a copy. Had he grown that callous or was he that convinced that I would not leave? I finally concluded that he was a very sick man.

An addiction to pornography is no different from any other addiction. When someone is an addict, they often forget about the detriment they are causing to themselves and those that love them. The source of the addiction becomes the driving force behind all of their decisions. In my husband's case, everything was heightened by his need to conceal his behavior. Each time I caught him, he appeared numb and callous, but I discerned something much deeper. There was an enormous guilt and shame that were working together to keep him in bondage.

Just as I was trying to sort through the data, the doorbell rang. My brother went to the door and came back to my room. He tapped my door and looked inside. "He's at the door. What do you want me to do? I will call the police. Just tell me what you want me to do." What could I do? Now my family was involved. I had not shared the totality of our situation with my brother. He likely thought we were just having a spat.

I created this situation. I made these choices. It wasn't fair for me to expose my family to this drama. I had to go home. There was no other viable option for me. I told my brother to let him in. My husband walked into my room and tried to hug me as if nothing was wrong. "I missed you," he said. I was in total disbelief! Who was this person? We sat and talked for a short while, and then I agreed to go home. I felt so helpless. I wanted to fight, but he had slowly removed all of my options.

We returned home and I tried to maintain the peace. I needed to start working on an exit plan, but that was going to be difficult. He had been injured on his job, so he was at home every day. All day.

I distracted myself by gathering the items for our taxes. I was hesitant about filing with him, but I did. I filed electronically, so I expected the refund to come rather quickly. When it didn't, I became concerned. I tried to call the IRS, but I could never get through. I kept asking him if he'd received anything, but his answer was always, "No."

After another month passed, I knew something was wrong. I knew something happened to our return. One day I went out to his truck to look for something I dropped. As I looked under the seat, I saw a piece of paper stuffed underneath the seat. I pulled it out. It was a letter from the IRS. They had applied our refund to an outstanding debt he and his former wife had, and he still owed $4000! He had lied, AGAIN! There was also another receipt stuffed under the same seat. It was for a nearby massage parlor. I checked the date and time. He had told me he was going to Home Depot! I gathered the documents and stuffed them into my pocket. I tried to look calm as I walked into the house.

Though my marriage was crumbling, I tried desperately to hold it together. I was ashamed that I was failing, and the fear of being less than perfect bound me to a marriage that was destroying me. One of the most difficult aspects of the entire ordeal is that we were pastors. Each Wednesday and Sunday we went to church. He ministered with all his might, preached against sin, and doted over me like I was a prized trophy. When we returned home, often before we even reached there, he morphed into someone else.

As a committed Christian, this was one of my greatest conflicts. I felt like such a hypocrite. I was covering for his indiscretions through my inaction and silence. He was not the man he pretended to be from the pulpit, and I knew it. I felt so guilty coming into God's presence. At times, I was angry at myself. I couldn't understand how I ended up in that situation. Though I felt defeated and broken, something inside of me refused to allow me to expose my reality. No one close to me had any idea the hell I was living in. I was living a lie.

Most of the people my husband encouraged me to talk to were women whose husbands were pastors who used porn, men who used porn, pastors who had cheated on their wives and been given "grace," or pastors who were involved in some other type of indiscretion. Obviously, none of those men were guiding him through repentance. Their wives' advice to me was usually centered on my need to pray and "cover the man of God." One pastor's wife even hinted at the fact that perhaps my marriage was struggling because I was too focused on the bar. She said I should just "put it on the back burner." It never occurred to her that all of the time, money, and effort I had expended in law school mattered. Though he was insulating me with individuals who sang this same chorus, my gut told me that living this way was wrong . . . very wrong.

I got my scores in May, and I had missed the required score by three points! Three points! I was so disappointed. It probably shouldn't have surprised me given all that was going on in my life, but I was depending on God for some type of breakthrough. I had been faithful. I was fighting for my marriage. I was keeping my husband's dirty little secret. The orphan spirit was in full throttle. I was trying very hard to be perfect, to be acceptable to God and everyone else around me. I convinced myself that God expected me to stay in my marriage. Still I wondered. Since I was doing all this for God, why wasn't He doing something for me? Why was He allowing my entire life to fall apart?

My husband never shared in my disappointment. In fact, he continued to say that God was punishing me. He said my pride had gotten out of control so God was using the failure to humble me. Until I submitted to God with my whole heart, he concluded, I would never succeed. As if my own self-doubts weren't enough to cripple me, I also had a partner and roommate who echoed and amplified those thoughts every day. I decided to take a break from the exam for a while. I would not sit for the next administration. Until something in my life situation changed, I was just wasting my time and money.

Later that summer, one of the ministers in our church, and his wife, left the church. He also announced that he was filing for divorce. My husband was livid. He forbade the minister to get a divorce. My husband told him if he went through with his plans, his license would be revoked. Worse still, my husband suggested that he was going to intervene.

"He was going to intervene. A pastor in an unstable marriage who was addicted to pornography was going to intervene?"

After they separated, some murmuring began among the parishioners. One day one of them called my husband. There was a rumor that the estranged minister had expressed a desire to come to church and shoot my husband! I suggested that he call the police, even his spiritual parents suggested the same, but he refused. He dismissed the murmurs and said he was going to have a meeting with the women who were involved in the gossip. I wanted no part of the debacle, so I stayed home. He came home and said he forbade them to continue any discussion about the issue. That was his solution—they should just stop talking about it!

I didn't concern myself with the issue because I finally had started my exit strategy. I began attending meetings at the battered women's shelter and discussed safety planning with the counselor. Attending the meetings was very embarrassing. I felt like I needed to conceal who I really was.

I couldn't tell everyone that I was a law student who used to help women escape their abusers. What would they think of me? The situation was very humbling. For the first few meetings, I basically cried every time it was my turn to share. The women were very supportive of me, but I felt guilty. They had left their abusers, but there I was, asking for emotional support, but each week I went home to mine!

I vacillated between leaving and staying. I did not want to admit that I had failed. I never planned to be divorced. In fact, I had always said I would NEVER get divorced. More importantly, I had convinced myself that my husband's issues were mine too. We were married, so I convinced myself that abandoning him would be wrong. Besides, none of our counselors seemed to suggest leaving as an option. My commitment to God was being used to keep me in bondage, both by others and myself. Still, I could not continue to deny the truth. My marriage was crumbling. I was drowning and there was no life preserver in sight.

We had gone through four counselors by this point and none of them were successful at helping us. It was during one of our sessions that I finally learned the truth about his pornography addiction. He had actually been watching pornography for over twenty years. He finally admitted that even his wife had caught him looking at it on their home computer. It is worth noting here that addictions are never about other people. Each time I caught him, I would tell myself maybe I should lose weight (I wasn't overweight), cook more, or be more sexually creative. I erroneously made his addictions somehow reflective of my deficiency. The revelation proved that the root cause was something larger. It wasn't about me at all.

He always got angry if the counselors ever confronted him, and no one seemed strong enough to shut him down. I was spending a lot of money on these sessions (we alternated paying for them), and we weren't making any progress. When I discovered that he also was engaging in conversations with women and deleting their calls, I stopped going altogether.

In my heart I knew our marriage was over. My primary issue was figuring out how I was going to get away from him. His emotions were often volatile and explosive. From my experience with him, I knew my exit would need to be calculated and well planned. I would not only need to leave him, I would also need a safe place to go.

I couldn't share the details of what was happening with anyone. Relations were getting better with my family, but we were still estranged. I couldn't tell my friends because I didn't really have any. My husband had been meticulous about narrowing my circle. First I had to cease conversation with anyone I ever dated, then it was men in general, from there it was anyone I knew who lived in Atlanta, and then it was all my friends because he said they were "too loose." In a matter of months, I found myself with no real outlet but him. This was by his design.

One summer day, we took a drive to run some errands. He went inside UPS and I waited in the car. I decided to write a couple of checks for my mother's estate while I waited for him. When I saw him approach the car, I began putting the checks away. I'm not really sure why I did that. I just always seemed to be on edge. He made me feel like everything I did was wrong, so I found myself always hiding, even when I was doing nothing wrong. This day, I was too slow. As he sat down in the car, he asked, "What were you just doing? Why did you put that checkbook away? Why are you always hiding from me?"

I took a deep breath, and then I asked him if he really wanted to know the answer. He answered in the affirmative, so I told him. I was honest about how scared I felt, how unstable he seemed, and how I didn't trust his ability to make responsible decisions for us. I should've stopped with the first one, but I didn't. I kept going. I was tired of being powerless. I was tired of not having a voice.

He began insulting me, calling me names, and telling me no one would ever want me. I focused on the road and tried to drown out his diatribe. Just as we were almost home, my phone rang. I quickly answered. I tried to sound calm and talked to my friend. When we arrived home, he stomped upstairs.

When I ended the call, I screamed upstairs to let him know I was off the phone. I have no idea why I volunteered for more of his railings. As he rushed down the stairs, he snatched my Bluetooth from my ear and threw it on the table. When I told him he hurt my ear, he chuckled as he said, "You'll be alright!" Then he grabbed my phone. He threw it onto the couch as he muttered, "I'm sick of you and this phone!" He picked up right where he left off from earlier. He screamed, cursed, and called me names I won't dare repeat. I started praying . . . aloud. I asked God for his intervention. I forbade the kingdom of darkness to invade my home. I commanded the spirit of rage to be still. I employed every tactic I had learned in my years of spiritual warfare. He paused and headed to the coffee maker. Foolishly thinking he was done, I stopped praying. He paused for a minute or two longer, and started again.

As he continued, I felt something in my gut telling saying, "Leave. You asked for an opportunity to get out. This is your moment. Get out!" I stood up and announced, "I'm leaving!" I grabbed my keys and purse as he walked to the sofa and picked up my phone. I asked for it, but he refused, so I asked again. He said, "If you want your phone, you get the police to get it for you." I grabbed my purse and walked out. As soon as I got into the car, I could hear my heart beating in my chest. Tears were streaming down my face. I could not do this by myself anymore. I needed help. I reached for my phone to call someone. Wait! I didn't have a phone! I pulled off anyway and decided my only recourse would be to go to the police station as he suggested.

I drove to the precinct and saw two police officers standing outside. I didn't realize until later that I was actually at the back of the building. I approached them cautiously and explained what had just transpired. They made a call for back up and called him to let him know they were coming with me to get my phone. After they hung up, they asked me my plans. I told them I wanted to leave. Even though that had been my apartment, I did not want to repeat the scenario of trying to get him to leave. I just needed to get away from him and have some peace.

They followed me home and parked their patrol car. Before we went in, they asked me details about weapons and his background. They also ran his license plate. Even with the policemen, I was terrified to approach my house again. All of my training taught that the most dangerous time for a victim is when she decides to leave. Even typing the word "victim" still bothers me. I would never have thought this would be my life. EVER.

The policemen went first. They tapped on the door and he opened it. They asked him what was going on, and he made it seem like a simple disagreement. When the officer told him that he had to return my phone, I began to relax. They also told him that I was leaving and he would be expected to stay seated while I went upstairs to gather some items. Thankfully, he complied.

I hurried upstairs to grab some of my things. How long would I be gone? What did I need? Where was I even going? My head was spinning with all the questions, but I could feel the strength of the adrenaline propelling me. I felt a surge of confidence when I thought to myself, "You are getting out alive. You finally did it! You're leaving him!" I knew that not all victims are as fortunate. God was being gracious to me, yet again.

I walked downstairs with my bags and tried not to look in his direction. I was finally free. I walked to my car with the policeman and got inside. They told me I should come by the precinct when I needed to come back for more of my personal items. The lead officer said, "You are making the right choice. These things rarely get better, but if you stick with your decision, you'll be a rare find." I didn't take offense to his words. He was right. This wasn't the first time I had tried to break free, but this time something inside felt different. I was leaving under different circumstances. The aggression had escalated. I felt certain I had heard God's voice. For months I had prayed to God, petitioning him to let me get out of the situation with my life. I firmly believed God had answered my prayer. I was finally moving forward.

6. ESCAPE ROUTE

WHERE DO YOU RUN WHEN
YOU'RE OUT OF OPTIONS?

I ended up driving to Atlanta to a hotel. On the way there, I called one of my friends from law school. She had recently gone through a divorce. She was very encouraging, and she forbade me to go back. I gave her the hotel information so someone would know where I was. I found a reasonable hotel off the beaten path and checked in. I just wanted to sleep. I was exhausted!

I slept soundly through the night, but as soon as I woke up again, my heart started racing. What was I going to do? I couldn't stay here forever. I didn't even have a job. I booked the hotel for two days, so I was covered for at least that long. I decided to go have lunch because I was famished. On the way back, my phone rang. I expected my husband, but it wasn't him. It was my brother! I wanted to decline the call. I had no idea what I was going to say to him. I had to make sure that he couldn't detect anything in my voice.

I made small talk about his day and his weekend plans. He didn't wait long before he asked, "So what are you up to? Where are you anyway?" I needed a way to answer the question that sounded honest. I told him I was just hanging out. That wasn't enough to deter him. He asked, "Hanging out? Where?" He had me. I was cornered. I blurted out, "At a hotel." He continued, "Well, what are you doing there? Where's your husband?" I told him my husband was at home, and I was alone because I had left him.

Everything about the conversation shifted. He demanded to know which hotel and whether I was okay. He also demanded that I check out immediately and come to his house. "You will not stay in any hotel. You will come here. You don't even have a job!" I reminded him how my husband had shown up before. I told him it wasn't safe. I shouldn't have said that because the reminder made his voice crack. "You're my little sister. I have to help you. What do you need me to do? Shall I put you on a plane? Just tell me." This exchange was something I had tried desperately to avoid. I didn't want him to worry. It was all my fault. I tried to reassure him that I was okay. I told him I needed to stay at the hotel another night to clear my mind and come up with a plan. He was hesitant, but he finally agreed. He made me promise to come over the next day.

I went to my brother's house the next day and ended up staying. The following Monday I decided to return home. I had left in such a rush; many of the items I needed were still at home. When I arrived, I called the police station. The dispatcher was very rude and uncooperative. She told me that no policeman would be escorting me to my house if my husband wasn't there because it was illegal.

Her behavior reminded me of an exercise we had done in law school. In one of the Family Violence clinic class sessions, we were each given an allowance. As we traveled through each scenario, there were common experiences a domestic violence victim might experience like a huge argument or fight, being forced out, or discovering molestation. At each juncture, there was a choice to be made concerning our finances. I remembered going through the exercise. At one point, I had used all of my "money," so I had to make a decision. I did not have enough for a hotel, so I had to choose either sleeping in the car with my kids or going back home to my abusive husband. Neither was a comfortable choice. Although the activity was just a simulation, its reality was a little too close to home. I started crying in class. At that moment I became acquainted with a level of desperation I had never felt before. I was forced to choose my safety or comfort. Now I was being told I could not even enter my own house without my husband. All of the drama makes going back seem a much easier choice.

Suddenly, I remembered that the original policeman had given me his card. I was so grateful. I reached out to him. The dispatcher finally agreed to send an officer, so I waited at a store nearby. My husband was not home when we got there, so I rushed upstairs. This time I had prepared a list. I feverishly packed the bags I brought. I was gathering the last few items when I heard a familiar voice downstairs. My husband was home!

I was very nervous, but I was relieved that the officers were there. They were there to protect me. They'd keep him at bay until I finished packing. WRONG! He walked right past them and headed upstairs. They didn't try to stop him. They didn't frisk him for weapons. NOTHING! I took a deep breath and told myself I would not show fear. I would not let him bully me anymore. He walked into the room and tried to hug me! I pushed him away. He looked shocked as he asked, "What's wrong?" What's wrong? Really? Did he just ask me that? I told him to move away from me so I could get my things. He complied, but he kept saying, "I just want to talk." I refused and rushed downstairs. He followed me all while the policeman just stood there looking at us. I didn't feel safe.

If my husband had been armed, I would have been defenseless against him. It's hard to believe that the policeman stood there like an observer, but it is true. Suddenly the fact that many women return to their abusers made perfect sense. If the police weren't going to protect them, who would? I felt an urgency to escape, so I grabbed my things and left.

I drove back to my brother's house. I was there for a week or so before my husband called demanding that I come home. I refused and flatly told him if he came there, I would call the police. I was not backing down this time. I was fighting for my life! After my second week there, my brother began asking about the bar exam. He said it was time for me to sit for the exam again. I could not believe what he was asking of me. He could not be serious. I was separated from my husband. I lived in someone else's house, and he thought now was the right time to sit for the biggest test of my life again?

He gave me his rationale. "You are here. You are safe and there are no distractions. No one is here during the day, so you have all day to study. You can do this. Now is the time. Besides, if you don't sign up, I am going to do it for you!" The idea sounded utterly ridiculous to me. Preparation for the bar is supposed to be an all-in thing. It is a high stakes test. There can be no distractions. I would have to devote myself to the process. I was not in the frame of mind to focus on that test.

After I pondered the idea a week or so, I decided that my brother was right. Obviously my life wasn't going to ever stop just so I could prepare. I would put all I had into my last try. If I was unsuccessful, I would just go make Big Macs.

I ordered a few study materials and gathered some books from a couple of classmates. Most of them had already become lawyers while I was testing, re-testing, and dealing with the drama of my married life!

I only had six weeks to prepare. I studied, but I was careful to take time off to rest and relax. I knew my body had been through a tremendous ordeal. I didn't take very many calls from my husband. Each one I accepted quickly turned toxic. I knew any interaction with him at this point would be counterproductive to my goal. I shut him out of my life. I told him if he wanted to save our marriage, he would have to get counseling and prove he had really changed. I also asked him to leave the apartment so I could come home. He flatly refused. I could not allow myself to be distracted with a fight; I decided to leave the issue for after the exam.

I spent the next two months with laser sharp focus. I didn't go to law school, invest $100,000, and leave my job and health insurance to fail. Whether I ever practiced law or not was of no consequence at that point. I resolved to finish. I began some serious self-talk. "This test will not defeat me. Life will not defeat me. I am a daughter of the most High God. I am an Overcomer. No good thing will He withhold from them who walk uprightly. The memory of the just is blessed. God will give me the knowledge and understanding He gave the Hebrew boys. I can do all things through Christ who strengthens me." I declared those words from my mouth several times daily and I willed myself to believe them!

I prepared for the test and paid all the necessary fees. Meanwhile there was more illness on the home front. My aunt had been in the hospital for over 12 months and her condition was worsening. The week of the exam, the hospital sent her home because there was nothing else they could do for her. I wanted to drive home to see her, but I knew I had to focus. It was game time.

I headed to my hotel the night before the exam. I took some food so I wouldn't have to leave the room. I checked in and went to bed extra early so I would be well rested. I woke up a little early, had oatmeal, and headed out to my car.

As I approached the car, I saw ants crawling all over my car door. Ants! They were everywhere. They had taken over my car. I quickly looked around to find their source and found a trail linked toward my trunk. I had forgotten my food container in the trunk, and those industrious little guys had found it! Ants were everywhere, but I had no time to waste, I had to get to my exam.

I said a quick prayer. I had specifically prayed Psalm 91 before leaving my room. As I drove and smashed ants, I wondered how this could be happening. This was my fourth attempt at taking this test. Was it a curse?

I made it to the exam about ten minutes after everyone else and quietly slid into my seat. I whispered another prayer and tried to calm myself. I was itching all over. My skin felt like ants were crawling on every inch. Finally, I calmed down and completed the exam.

Once I completed the test, I decided to make some decisions about the tornado spiraling in my personal life. I needed to move forward with my life. My aunt had passed away on the last day of my exam, but no one told me until after it was over. There was no down time. Her funeral was scheduled for that weekend.

Even though my husband and I were separated, I fully expected him to come. My aunt was very fond of him, and I was pretty sure our separation wasn't known by everyone. He never showed up. A few people asked me where he was. I told them he was at home. Those who didn't know something was awry were definitely put on notice then.

After the funeral, I decided to go home. I needed to pick up my mail and I wanted to make a final decision about the course my marriage would take. For some strange reason, I still thought my marriage could be saved. He was very surprised to see me, and he acted very cool. Although he pretended to be happy to see me, something just seemed off.

Although we ended up going to the movies, we felt like strangers. When it was time for bed, he wanted to sleep with me, but I was very conflicted. He was my husband. We were still married. My body belonged to him. Or did it? Was pornography the look on a woman to sleep with her that Jesus spoke of? Was that really adultery? What if he had been with someone else while I was away? I was an emotional wreck. I stayed overnight but I decided doing anything sexual would only cloud my judgment even further. He was not happy, but I left him to deal with that. I had made my decision. My marriage was over.

When I returned to Atlanta, I started searching for a Christian counselor. I found an excellent one. She was quite adept at helping me honestly unpack my feelings. I wasn't too happy about that, but I knew it was needed. It was time for the mask to come off. I had feigned strength for far too long. It was time for me to be transparent with God, her, and myself.

I was deeply broken. The cascade of trials had come like rapid fire from a semi-automatic weapon. I was still standing, but I was deeply wounded. If I didn't get to triage soon, I likely would not make it.

My counselor strongly encouraged me to plant myself in a new church, but I just couldn't. I didn't skip church, but I didn't plant myself anywhere. I found it difficult to trust anyone. I had been hurt terribly by the people who knew my husband and me, and most of them were leaders in the church. Even though he was the one who was in sin, everyone rallied around him and treated me like I had a scarlet "A" on my chest!

After a few sessions, my counselor instructed me to apply Matthew 18 to my marriage situation. In Matthew 18:15-17, Jesus taught the church how we are to deal with conflict.

> Moreover if your brother sins against you, go and tell him his fault between you and him alone. If he hears you, you have gained your brother. But if he will not hear, take with you one or two more, that 'by the mouth of two or three witnesses every word may be established.' And if he refuses to hear them, tell it to the church. But if he refuses even to hear the church, let him be to you like a heathen and a tax collector.

Since I had expressed my conflict to him with no results, it was time to bring in witnesses. I contacted a couple I trusted. They were pastors, and they knew both of us. They asked me to share my story, so I did. I figured they could not help if I wasn't honest with them. After I shared my ENTIRE story, they told me they needed to pray about it. They promised to get back to me.

They never did.

There was another pastor and his wife, an older couple, who we had grown very close to. The husband had actually been one of our very first counselors. I trusted them and their wisdom. I didn't have natural grandparents anymore, so I looked to them to fill that role. I loved them and tried to honor them every chance I got. I volunteered on small projects they needed help with, even though I was already helping my husband pastor a church. When everything started falling apart with my ex-husband, they rallied around him and shunned me. Even though he and I were in their Bible study every week for over three years, they did not even reach out to me. No prayer call, no call of concern. Nothing! Sadly, I had to return to my counselor and tell her I had no one to call as my "witnesses."

I quickly learned that some aspects of our life as pastors were like a gang. I had been "jumped in," and I was expected to follow the rules. I was called to protect my husband, keep his secrets, and pretend everything was okay. I was a first lady and I needed to understand how hard it was to be a pastor. Men would be men, right. Even pastors. Those were the things that were communicated to me. Through the alienation of our "friends," I learned the culture code. I was expected to stand by him, regardless. If I did not, I was finished. No one would call, text, or visit me again.

When people gave me the scriptures about God and divorce, I could sense their disapproval of me. You need to go home. He's a pastor! First ladies don't do that! Cover him! It doesn't matter what he's done! My husband did that too, but I didn't leave him! Have you fasted? You should pray more! You just need to give him more sex! Yes, I heard it all.

All of the judgment and criticism made me ashamed of my decision. Had I done enough? Was it really my fault? What was wrong with me? Right before I separated from my husband, I had begun to function in ministry. I was teaching Bible study, leading women's small groups, and handling parts of our Sunday service. As a matter of fact, I was scheduled to be ordained as co-pastor two months later. Our separation stopped all those things. Nobody wanted to hear my gift anymore.

The next week, I texted our pastor and asked her if we could talk. I hesitated to call her because she lived thousands of miles away. Furthermore, I feared that she would be like all the other church people—I thought she might shun me too. She agreed to talk to me, and we spoke later in the week. My husband had always told me that he was sharing everything with her. He wasn't. She had heard nothing about the porn or the separation. I'm pretty sure she was in a difficult situation. She was just being brought in, but the marriage was technically already done. She told me she would need to speak with him. She promised to schedule a three way conference call later in the week.

We ended up having the conference call and the conversation confirmed everything I knew in my gut. My husband didn't deny any of the things I shared. When it was his turn to share his side, he refused to talk. He said the Lord told him to forgive and move forward. The truth was he was unwilling to say the untruthful things he's shared with her with me on the phone. During our marriage he had become quite skillful at disparaging my character. He told many of our friends and church associates that I was cheating on him and didn't know how to be a wife. I was pretty sure his conversations with her had been no different.

Now that the three of us were on the phone together, the truth was being revealed. She expressed her desire that we work on the marriage. She reminded us that God's heart is always for reconciliation. She emphasized the fact that we would both have to be willing to put forth the effort. He was resolutely defiant. He was unrepentant. He told her I needed to get over the past and move forward. He simply said I needed to move on.

Consequently, our pastor said she could not demand that I stay in the marriage. Based on what we shared, she, too, believed I had biblical grounds for divorce. He became enraged and accused her of siding with me. We ended the conversation without any semblance of a "meeting of the minds."

We had been married for a little less than two years. Every day I had prayed and hoped for his deliverance and peace in our home. Neither came. I cried, screamed, and sat in bewilderment. How could this be happening . . . to me? We were Christians! Wasn't this supposed to work? I didn't believe in divorce! Nevertheless, there was no denying the obvious. My marriage was over. I could not return to my life as it was, and nothing had changed. It was time to face the truth. My marriage was over. After four months of grueling work with a Christian counselor and a failed intervention with our pastor, I couldn't waste any more time. I filed for divorce.

Thirty-one days later, my marriage was dissolved. A judge's stroke of the pen was all it took to make it as if it never happened. With one singular decision, I lost my marriage, my home, my two step-children, my church family, and by all accounts-my ministry. The dreams I had for our powerful deliverance ministry were shattered. I was left to face the accusations, the questions, and the hushed silences when I entered the room. My new reality was that I was now a divorcee. A *former* pastor's wife. A Christian. A divorcee. The three descriptions together seemed like an anomaly.

7. COURSE CORRECTION
HOW DOES GOD SHIFT YOUR TRAJECTORY?

After my divorce was finalized, I began the process of starting over. My ex-husband finally vacated our home and I was able to go back. I actually spent a month there before I decided to move. It was a surreal feeling being there alone. The last two years of my life had been spent there with him. Several times I sat on the bed and just stared at the ceiling.

All of my dreams for my marriage were over. Grieving the loss felt like death. I used the month to process some of my thoughts and pack all my belongings. It would be wiser for me to permanently move in with my brother, whether I wanted to or not.

I finally packed everything and got ready for moving day. My brother came to my house and helped me finalize everything. The next morning, I put all my things in storage and made the permanent move. At first, it was extremely challenging. I was used to having a place of my own. Slowly, however, I began to heal and establish a comfortable schedule. One day I received a circular in the mail about a tour to Israel with Jenetzen Franklin. I had always wanted to take a pilgrimage to Israel, but I figured it would come much later in life. I tried to register for the trip, but I had missed the deadline. I was devastated. I really needed a break from my life.

I started establishing a new life for myself. I attended conferences, listened to sermons, and tried to enjoy myself. I looked forward to starting my new career, and I decided to put ministry in the back of my mind. I was perfectly content to live my life and enjoy the spiritual gifts of others. I had been through a traumatic series of events. I felt entitled to a break from leading or teaching anyone. Besides, I was a woman who was also divorced. No one would want me anywhere near their pulpit. The shame of being a divorcee followed me, so I stopped preaching. I stopped teaching. I became a church hopper who just warmed the pew. Rejection made sure I felt ashamed of my decision to divorce and tried to ensure that I would be too fearful to start again.

In Exodus 3, Moses was tending the flock on the back side of the mountain. He had started a new life. Memories of life in Egypt were long past. He was minding his own business living his life when suddenly:

> The Angel of the LORD appeared to him in a blazing flame of fire from the midst of a bush; and he looked, and behold, the bush was on fire, yet it was not consumed. So Moses said, "I must turn away and see this great sight—why the bush is not burned up." When the LORD saw that he turned away to look, God called to him from the midst of the bush and said, "Moses, Moses!" And he said, "Here I am."

The Creator of Moses' destiny calls to him from a burning bush. God reminds him of his lineage and His divine connection to his forefathers. Then God proceeds to reveal the reason for His appearance. The children of Israel are oppressed. They have been crying out to Him, and He has come to answer. Well, actually he has come to reveal the answer. Moses is God's answer. He plans to use him to address the oppression of the Israelites.

Like Moses, I left my former life and started another one. I planned to lead a normal life and just fit in. Never mind my purpose or what God had actually planned. After all that had happened, I felt sure I had missed him along the way. I would just live out the remainder of my life under the radar. Things would be much easier that way. That plan might have actually worked if I had stayed out of prophetic churches, but something kept drawing me there.

Shortly after filing for divorce, I went to an Apostles and Prophets Conference in Atlanta. The experience was electric. As each pastor delivered the Word, the intensity increased. Though I was facing great difficulty, I could sense in my gut that something was about to change. Friday afternoon, there was a session entitled, "The Father's Throne Room." I had no idea what that could mean, but the title alone had me interested.

When we all returned from lunch, the pulpit was transformed. It had become an altar. There was a large crown on the front table. The crown was covered in bright, glimmering jewels. Beautiful, sequined jeweled cloths covered the table. They were arrayed in every imaginable color. The lights were low and worship music filled the air. Everyone hurried into the room. Expectancy filled the space. I noticed that people brought their blankets and pillows. Some even had their prayer shawls. I was getting excited, too, but I was also very nervous. What had I signed up for?

The leader walked onto the stage and began to give us instructions. We were going to engage in a process called "soaking." Thankfully I had been introduced to the concept a few months prior. Basically, soaking is Biblically based meditation. Most people use recorded instrumental music; there are even artists who create soaking music as their specialty. The music is played softly while the individual worships God. The worship takes many forms—some pray, some read their Bibles, others meditate, some simply talk to God, and others sit still and wait for God to speak to them. I had actually soaked many times over the summer and found deep, convergent experiences with God each time.

Most of the time, I lost track of time as I lay quietly on the floor, on my face in the presence of God. I thought I was simply enjoying His presence, but God had been doing much more; He was training me for the warfare I would endure.

The leader instructed us to find a comfortable place to relax. Anxious conference attendees grabbed their coats, blankets, and cloths and scurried around the sanctuary. We were preparing to hear from God, and we were like little children on Christmas Eve! I was excited to hear from God, but I was also anxious about what he might say. There were parts of my heart that were very fractured, and I was pretty confident I didn't want to deal with them.

Her next instructions were the most intriguing. The music would play softly as we soaked. The leader prepared to pray and walk the room as we rested. As the Holy Spirit instructed, she would place the "mantles," the sequined cloths, over us. A mantle is a covering or an important role or responsibility that passes from one person to another. According to Wikipedia, mantles were used in the Bible to convey authority and confirm a calling from God.

Our leader instructed us to relax so we could be prepared to receive. Later, after the period of soaking was over, she would deliver prophecy about each mantle's significance to the individuals who received them. Now, I was really scared! Would I receive a mantle? Would God talk to me? What would He say? All these questions rushed through my mind as I set to prepare my area. My mind wandered and questioned, so I couldn't really concentrate. Finally, my heart stopped racing and I began to relax.

The songs were tailored specifically for the experience. Each song built on the intensity of the prior one. I chose to lie flat on my blanket, and I placed my prayer cloth over me. I started to talk to God about the conflict I felt. I figured I should begin the conversation, so I could control the flow.

It's ironic. Even in the presence of God I felt the need to be in control. I wanted to hear from Him, but I was also scared to hear what He had to say. I was honestly seeking for answers to the very difficult season I was in. I talked about some of the things I lost, but I could almost feel myself pulling away from Him.

Times of intimacy with God can be challenging. He begins to reveal barriers in your heart that He wants to address. All the normal defense mechanisms of humanity come to the surface. Some try to deny them, some get angry, some pretend the issue lies with someone else. All of these strategies are futile. There is no hiding ANYTHING in the present of an omniscient God. In response to my resistance, I sensed him pulling away.

I'm sure this is difficult, even impossible to believe. The idea of God pulling away seems unconscionable. Yet, it is true. God is a person. He has feelings. He mourns, grieves, and gets angry. He has emotions. He desires to be accepted by us and welcomed into our hearts. Intimacy with us is the driving force of his heart. Still, He wants to be wanted.

I began to cry. I wanted desperately to feel the intimacy and closeness that He approached to offer, yet my pain was a very real barrier to the ability to be completely open and transparent with Him. I quietly sobbed.

I was embarrassed. I was too proud to receive the healing I needed. This was going nothing like I expected. I had anticipated a soft, fuzzy experience with God. I thought he would comfort me and tell me He understood how pitiful I felt. I longed for him to focus on the issues with the Christians who had hurt me and the pain I received from my husband. None of that was His focus. He was gently tugging at my heart. He was beckoning me to open it. It didn't seem to matter that I was hurting. He didn't seem deterred by my resistance. His message was clear. He wanted . . . me.

I was not prepared to lay my heart bare before him. I

had been through so much trauma. I wasn't sure what might come out of my heart if I opened it up to him. I continued to lie there on my face and tried to focus on the music. I wasn't ready to be exposed. I needed a distraction. As God continued to petition for my heart, it seemed like there were only the two of us. The music seemed muted and the stillness made it feel like all the air had been sucked out of the room.

Just as I settled into meditation on the words of the song, I felt something being placed over me. Almost immediately, it was like a dagger was being removed from my heart. I was frozen. I could not move. Though I wasn't sure exactly what, I knew something pretty significant was taking place. The stabbing pain in my heart only lasted for a few seconds. Although, it quickly subsided, I felt like I had been in a war zone. I let out a deep breath and succumbed to sleep.

I woke up when I heard the leader talking. She was rousing us from our slumber. Many others had fallen asleep, but now it was time for God to give us revelation. It was time to receive the prophecy concerning my mantle. I slowly turned over and, for the first time, saw the mantle that had been placed over me. It was bright red and it glittered as though imbued with flecks of gold. I sat up and made sure my name tag was visible. That was probably the only coherent thing I was able to accomplish in the entire time period! The leader began to circulate around the room. Not everyone in the room had received mantles—only the individuals Holy Spirit led her to.

I listened intently as she shared Holy Spirit's message to the others. As each moment passed, I became apprehensive. I wanted to hear what God had to say to me. I was very curious about the mantle I received, but I was also afraid. Finally, the leader approached me. I tried to calm by breathing. My heart was prepared, or so I thought. I lifted my head and listened intently. As the leader approached me, she called my name. I sat up straight as she began to speak:

My daughter, I am covering you anew in my blood today. For the enemy has come against you and has battled and tried to come in and tried to even steal and rob some things that were destined as part of your inheritance. But today I have drawn the blood line against him that when he sees you, he will see my blood. And no longer will he be able to come and rob and steal and even try to kill. He will no longer have access for I have decreed, 'Enough is enough!' Now is the time for the turnaround. It is time for the things to begin to move in the way I have decreed in your book. For there are many things I have written in the chapters of your life. Daughter, your best days lie ahead! So do not look at that which has come before, but look at how I am leading you in this hour. And know, My Precious One, that You are protected; You are covered! And when the enemy sees how I have covered you, He will scatter seven ways for he will not be able to touch you. For if he does, he will burn. For my passion, my fire is upon you. I have called you-- even for this hour. Daughter, you will walk in the miraculous. And it will start with you, and then it will spread and spread and spread. For these hands were destined for warfare. So now is your hour, it is coming now. So, Daughter, Prepare yourself! Consecrate your heart and know that I am leading you into a victory that will bring joy and release and will bring a GREAT, GREAT glory to MY NAME!

Tears streamed down my face. I could not say a word. God had spoken. Just as God spoke to Moses at the burning bush, God had spoken to me. His words proved that he had not forgotten me. My life was still part of His plan. He still wanted to use my life. My ministry wasn't over after all. God

97

saw my pain, my struggle against the enemy's attacks, and my desperation. He had come to deliver a word of hope and restoration into my life. Despite all that had occurred, God still had an awesome plan for my life!

When we receive a word of prophecy, we are often taken aback by the tremendous divide between our current reality and God's revelation of where he plans to take us. In our finite reasoning and perspective, we cannot begin to understand how the words could ever be possible. We wonder and reason if the things he reveals could ever occur. In these moments of wonder, it is helpful to remember the omniscience of God. He speaks to us from our future. He is innately aware of not only where we are but where He intends to take us. The separation between our finite minds and God's omniscience is precisely the reason prophetic ministry is needed. Prophecy opens the heart to an understanding of what God desires for our destiny. It allows us to begin to see ourselves as He sees us and often gives us a strategy on how to get there.

This is the power of the prophetic word. It encourages, edifies, and strengthens the hearer. It unlocks destinies and reveals a snapshot of God's viewpoint. You begin to hear how God sees you, and your life is transformed forever.

The next day, I received personal prophecy concerning writing a book and sitting on councils of influence. Everything seemed so different from what I saw in front of me. Fear began to creep in. I wasn't as afraid of the prophecies not coming true as how my life would change if they did. Today, wherever you are, you are reading a book that was birthed through a prophetic word I received after one of the lowest seasons in my life. God is intentional!

8. WORLD CHANGERS

HOW DO YOU START OVER WITH NO ROADMAP?

I have always struggled with fear whenever I am faced with a new opportunity or challenge. I knew it would try to stop me again if I didn't take the initiative to fight against it. One of the speakers at the conference spoke about the spirit of fear and how it stops our destiny. The sermon was powerful and it resonated with me deeply. I discovered that his church was hosting a conference the following month. I knew I was going to need help moving forward. If everything the prophet said about me was true, I was going to be doing a lot of shifting. I wasn't quite sure if I would be able to do any of that on my own.

I checked the dates and registered for the conference. The timing was extremely significant. My bar exam results would also be released while I was there. In the interim, I planned to start working on ideas for branding my new identity. I was no longer a victim. It was time for every aspect of my life to begin to reflect the change.

I also decided to peruse some nearby church sites to look for support groups. One of the churches had an interesting group for women who were married to Christian men who were also sexual addicts. I know. The two titles seem strange together. They should. I was quite hesitant about signing up for the group. Frankly, I did not want to revisit the pain. I needed to move forward. After a little coaching from my counselor, I signed up for the group. I needed to be around other women who understood what I had been through. Maybe I could also help them with their journeys.

The first meeting was somewhat awkward for me. After all, this wasn't a cooking group, a group for soccer moms, or a book club. This was a group that no one wanted membership in. We were part of group that we would never have chosen for ourselves. The thing we had in common was our pain, trauma, and dealing with betrayal. Our husbands were all addicted to pornography or women or men or sex or both. Though their addictive behaviors had taken them to different extremes, the fact still remained—we were all married to men who had a deep dark secret further complicated by the idea that they claimed to be Christians. All of us were deeply traumatized and broken by the events. My membership was even trickier. How would I truly be a part when I really wasn't? I was no longer fighting for my marriage. I had thrown in the towel. I had walked away. I would have to trust Holy Spirit to help me navigate these peculiar waters.

The ladies ended up helping me more than I realized. They had all been married for years, and the vicious cycle with their husbands continued. Their stories prevented me from giving myself any false hope. Their pain and trauma kept the reality prominently in my face. Remaining married to my husband would be no stroll in the park. The ladies' husbands had committed their offenses time and time again. Though the class wasn't actually designed to help women leave their husbands, that's pretty much what it had done for me. I knew I could never live like this for five, ten, or twenty years.

I attended classes every week, and the content we completed was grueling. I did not want to think about everything that had happened. I didn't want to face my own role in contributing to my life. The homework forced me toward that realization. I finally had to admit that one of the reasons I'd stayed was to maintain appearances with others. Holy Spirit brought Proverbs 29:25 to my remembrance.

Fear of man brings a snare, but whoever trusts in and puts his confidence in the Lord will be exalted and safe.

Ouch! My concern for how others saw me had kept me in bondage. More importantly, my dependence on their opinions meant I didn't really trust God. God dealt with that. Very strongly.

Another issue that Holy Spirit began to unpack was pride. That sin was closely connected to the fear issue. They were operating together to thwart my purpose and destiny. I enjoyed being a pastor's wife. I liked being upfront, on the platform, with the microphone, and I liked the privilege the position afforded me. When we went to other churches, we were always escorted up front. When I met someone new, I got to announce myself as the pastor's wife.

My preoccupation with status and recognition kept me entangled in a nightmare. I had to finally admit the truth—I wasn't just living a lie to protect him. I was also protecting me—my image and people's perception of me. Part of the reason I stayed was for the celebrity of it all.

We see it all the time with men who are well-known or in positions of power. If they are caught in some public sin or indiscretion, their wives rarely leave. They attend the press conferences together. The wives show off their new "I'm so sorry" trinkets and they move on. Just like I had done. Those were very difficult truths to swallow, but Holy Spirit made sure I got it. I would not be moving forward with half-truths or lies. The veil was coming off. God required that I accept the truth . . . about me.

Time arrived for the new conference, and I was very

excited. Many of the former attendees I met told me that my life would never be the same. I was looking forward to starting my new life, so I welcomed the change. The conference was more than I could ever have imagined. The worship sets were passionate, powerful, and purging. I gave myself fully to the experience and found myself feeling much freer after every service. They also provided time slots for prophetic words and deliverance. I did not have a slot, but a girl I met gave me hers. The prophetic word I received was very detailed and intense.

The second day of the conference was also bar exam score release day. I woke up that morning energized yet nervous. Scores were not supposed to be released until after 4:00, so I had all day to wait. I was determined not to focus on the scores; after all, I had taken the test months ago and the scores were already recorded. I would try my best not to think about it.

The morning service was electric. The power of the Holy Spirit was so strong that the pastor struggled to preach. Every time he tried to talk, he began speaking in tongues. It was clear that Holy Spirit planned to control the service. The second session was just as powerful.

Finally it was time to break for lunch. I needed to locate my friends, so I took out my cell phone. I had a text message. When I opened it, it said, "Congratulations, Girl! You did it! You passed!" Wait? Had I just read the text correctly? Results weren't supposed to be released until four. My hands started shaking and I couldn't breathe. I was in a foreign city with thousands of people I didn't know. I needed to confirm it. But how? Two girls I met in the conference invited me to go eat with them. When we stopped at their hotel, I rushed to the hotel conference center. I needed to see my name on the list for myself. Had I finally beaten this elusive test? Was I really a lawyer? I needed to know.

I sat at the computer and typed in the URL for the state bar site. When I got the login screen, my brain froze. I couldn't remember my login credentials! My hands were still shaking. I tried to think, but my brain was in a fog. Finally I remembered that the list was public.

I googled "Georgia bar exam results" and found the link. The list was alphabetized. I scrolled quickly through the early letters. When I came to the M's I started slowing down. I had been through the process before and my name was always missing. I scrolled down and there it was! Adrienne Denise Mayfield. I had passed the Georgia bar.

Things were finally turning around. A tear rolled down my cheek. Who would I call? Who could I share the news with? Almost immediately my mind thought of my parents. I wanted to share the news with them. I texted my brother the link and waited a few minutes. He didn't respond, so I called him. I asked him why he hadn't responded to my text. He grabbed his phone and started to read my text. When he clicked on the link, he started screaming, "You did it! You did it! Adrienne, Oh, my God!"

I went to find my lunch mates, and I shared my news. Neither of them knew me, and they didn't seem very happy. That was disappointing, but I was unfazed. I had worked too hard for this moment. I was like Diana Ross, "I'm coming out! I want the world to know! Got to let it show!" I even told my waitress and when we returned to the conference, I told the first six people I passed. I was beyond excited!

When I received my results, I reflected on the ants that covered my car. I had considered their appearance to be the sign of something ominous. Holy Spirit immediately brought the words of Proverbs 6:6-8 to my remembrance:

> Go to the ant, you sluggard! Consider her ways and be wise, which, having no captain,

> Overseer or ruler, Provides her supplies in the summer, *and* gathers her food in the harvest.

The ants were a signal that God was granting me wisdom to pass the test. God was with me. His providential grace carried me through adversity and an ant infestation. As a matter of fact, I received the exact score I asked him for.

As soon as I returned home, I began arranging my swearing-in ceremony. Thankfully, I was able to get the judge I'd always dreamed about. My brother and one of my friends from law school came to the ceremony, and they took lots of pictures. Afterwards, my brother even took me to lunch at my favorite restaurant. Things were finally beginning to shift. I was on Cloud Nine!

9. A NEW NORMAL

HOW DO YOU KEEP YOUR
WOUNDS FROM BLEEDING OUT?

I spent most of my spare time praying and reading my Bible. I knew I needed strength for the journey that lay ahead of me. One day, I was listening to a teaching on Periscope. The minister was talking about the spirit of Jezebel and her attempts to abort our promises from God. The teaching was very interesting. When he finished, he said he was going to prophesy to some people. He called my name and began:

> Adrienne, this is a season of picking up for you. This is a season where it's time for you to pick up where you left off. You've left things behind. No more going back. No more going in circles, for this is a time to recover the gold and to recover the things that have been stolen from you. I am leading you to the field of flowers for you are my radiant flower. I am connecting you to those other flowers I've called you to. Yes, this is your season of connecting with the burning bush. So I sent Moses on behalf of Israel, so I send you out into the field where the other flowers are. Those I've called you to prune, those I've called you to grow, those I've called for you to water, even those I've called you to divinely connect to. I'm going to shoot you out like a rocket. I'm releasing a fire of ignition in your life. I'm opening every single gift that I've given to you for I have blessed you with spiritual blessings in heavenly

places. My spiritual blessings are going to come on you, daughter, like never before. For you will know me as your good, good father. It is your time to reclaim your inheritance. This is a season of reclaiming your stake—reclaiming your plot of land. Arise against those giants that have risen in your land. I hear the words, "What has happened to you?" There are people who are going to say what has happened to you! They will come in the spirit of Jezebel disguising themselves by being sarcastic. They will try to make you feel ashamed, like you're doing the wrong thing. But I am lifting my hand on behalf of the humble. And even as you have humbled yourself, I am moving my strong hand in this hour. You will not be deterred by words that have been spoken against you in the past, words that have been spoken to make you give up your inheritance. This is a season of reclaiming for I have not forgotten about you. This is a launching into your call. This is a season where I have called you to the holy mountain. So often you have heard the sounds of hell. You have listened to the sounds of terror that made you draw back. Sounds that made you discouraged, sounds that made you want to quit, sounds of condemnation. But today I shoot my arrows at the sounds of condemnation. I am releasing sounds of righteousness, peace, and joy from my heavenly throne—sounds of the river of life into your life. My plans are here for you. My assignments are here for you.

I had been toying with the idea for a book about my story. As soon as I heard the words, "Connecting with the Burning Bush," I knew that was the title. God specifically used that prophetic word to reveal the title of this book. He also used the word to remind me that he was calling me to minister to women using my testimony. That revelation was both exciting and scary. My story shared many things that would put others in an unfavorable light. Telling the truth about my marriage would be liberating but it also could be dangerous. Still, I knew I needed to share my story. I begin to focus on the fact that God had promised to be with me. I would not be afraid.

Thanksgiving was pretty calm. I was finally getting settled into the idea that I was no longer married. Anticipation about my next steps began to plague me. Where would I work? Where would I live? How would I move forward?

One day, I lay on my bedroom floor crying out to God. I asked Him why he wasn't giving me specific directions. I had learned part of His plan for my future from the prophecies I received, but I had no clue how to get from here to there. I wept in His presence and opened my heart to Him. He responded. He told me that the next few months would be a healing season for me. He confirmed that He intended to use my story to heal other women, but I had to heal first. He didn't want me to bleed out. I understood perfectly.

Though my marriage was over, I was exhausted—spiritually, emotionally, and physically. I needed to take some time to rest and restore. One of the prophetic words I received during that period expressed that same idea. God said, "I am asking you have a Sabbath. To rest. To pull and get restored." That's not at all what I wanted to hear at the time. My future had been on hold. I wanted to get a job in my new career, move into my own place, and start over, but God knew something I was not yet aware of. It would take months to heal.

Over the next few months, God took me through intensive heart surgery. He went deep with the scalpel of His Word. He challenged all my beliefs about Him, the church, and me. It was gut wrenching work. I cried a lot. I prayed a lot. Several times I wanted to just give up. God was much more committed to the process than was; He wouldn't let me go. He pursued me and faithfully sent nuggets of encouragement through prophetic words and in my times of personal worship.

In December I attended a Sisterhood Conference for women. It was cathartic being with other women. We weren't there licking our wounds, bemoaning our fates, or bashing the men in our lives or the lack thereof. Instead we sang, laughed, prayed, and cried together. I was beginning to heal, and it felt liberating.

One of the ladies mentioned that she was having issues with headaches. During our break, I headed outside for some fresh air. As I was walking out the door, I saw the lady. Almost simultaneously, I heard a small voice, "Go lay hands on her. Ask me to heal her." I knew the voice well enough by now to know it was Holy Spirit. There was no question about it. The problem was the fact that I didn't know her; she didn't know me, and people don't usually just lay hands on each other outside church. I know we should, but it's not very common. After a few seconds of hesitation, my feet started moving. I approached her and asked if I could pray for her. To my surprise, she said, "Yes! Please do." Right there, in the backyard of the retreat location, I laid hands on her and commanded the headaches to go. When I finished, she started grinning. "My head isn't hurting!" Thank God it worked. She probably had more faith than I did. Little did I know, this miracle was only the beginning.

One Friday night in particular, I went to a service at a church nearby. Service was good. I enjoyed worship and the teaching was excellent. I had never once considered leaving church altogether; I had just decided that leading and being in a pulpit were probably over for me. After service was over, we were encouraged to stay for the prophetic encounter session. I hadn't received a prophetic word in a while, so I decided to stay. The prophetic team circulated around the room, each member of the team taking a turn. Just as the session was ending, one of the prophets came to my side of the room. She pointed to me! She asked me to stand and then she began,

> Daughter, I say to you that you have been like the woman with the issue of blood. You pressed and you pressed your way through the crowds. You pressed your way through the circumstances. You pressed your way through your situations. And know that smile, even that smile that you wear on the outside, many don't know the hurt and the brokenness on the inside but I say to you, daughter, that I'm doing a work in you now. That smile that you wear on the outside is beginning to match what's on the inside. Because there is so much on the inside of you and as you've pressed, I allowed you to go through these things. There were some things I wanted to remove and some things I wanted to add. There is birthing that is coming forth. I have taught you how to push; I've taught you how to persevere in this season. Yes, it has been rough. You wanted to quit, but you kept pushing; you kept going; you kept coming. So, Daughter, I am calling that intercessor on the inside of you to rise up the warrior I called you to be. Yes, many ostracized you, many persecuted you, many looked over you, many even spoke negative words over you saying it could not be, it would not be, but Daughter, I say it is, it can be, and it shall be because you are one with a voice. And I have called you to be one that will speak and minister to women. Yes, from the brokenness the hurt and the pain, from the shame. But know that I, even as I am healing you, I have called you to be one that will be

used to heal and deliver through the love and the compassion because you know the hurt. You know the pain. But now it is time for you to begin to experience my joy and my love like you have never experienced it before. Oh, yes, I'm coming to visit you. I'm coming to overshadow you with my love, my peace, and with my glory. And yes, even pertaining to your finances— yes, you lost some stuff, but I am getting ready to bless you. I'm getting ready to expand you. Yes you were alright sitting behind the scenes and just relaxing, but Daughter, know that I have given you a voice and you must speak. And you must speak forth the Word. And even as you give your testimony-Watch me heal! Watch me deliver! And every time you tell the testimony, deliverance will come forth through you. And I see you, you were even like David. You had to encourage yourself many days but know that the encouragement that you rendered unto yourself and even unto others when you were going through, I am sending those that will pour into you and love on you, but better yet, I'm coming to pour my love out on you.

Wow! AGAIN? I was enjoying my sabbatical. I found great pleasure in feasting on the ministry gifts of others. Didn't God understand that I was wounded? Didn't He care that I had been hurt very badly by people in the church. Was He really planning to use me to bless His people? I kinda liked being in the background. It felt safe and almost guaranteed I wouldn't be wounded again. Although I was comfortable and settled, apparently I was very much out of place.

Toward the end of the month, I headed back to Athens to take care of some business. On the way there, I felt a funny feeling in my stomach. I couldn't quite put my finger on it. After I arrived, my sister called me. She told me that a young lady from my hometown was in the hospital.

She wanted me to go pray for her. Since I was already there, I decided to pay her a visit.

She had been in and out of hospitals for months, and the doctors were scratching their heads. They could find no medical reason for her inability to digest her food. Still, every time she would try to eat or drink something, she would throw up. She'd gone to several hospitals and seen every type of specialist in the field; nothing was working. I wasn't sure what was wrong with her, but I knew it was not God's will for her to be sick.

Something about the way some Christians deal with illness seems off. It is not consistent with Scripture. We say we are going to pray for the sick, but Jesus never prayed for the sick. He healed the sick! I wonder if we could shorten our sick and shut in lists if we only had the faith to believe for healing of every sick person we encounter.

I drove to the hospital and prayed all the way there. I asked Holy Spirit what He wanted me to do. When I drove into the parking garage, I began to sense that something very serious lay ahead of me. I parked my car and walked up the stairs. I knocked on the hospital door, and peeked inside. The young lady opened her mouth in disbelief. She looked at her friend and said, "Can you believe it? Can you believe she's here? I asked God to let you come pray for me!" I couldn't believe it. I was the answer to someone's prayer!

She shared some things about her condition with me. She was weak and very thin. While I was there, she threw up a couple of times. Her friend and I had to use the trashcan to catch it and try to keep her from passing out. Over the next several weeks, I visited her several times. We laughed, talked, and prayed. The more she shared her life, the more freedom she gained. Still, we were in intense warfare. I began to notice a pattern. Whenever certain people would call, she would throw up and get sick.

Her doctor ordered psychological tests, but I knew that wasn't the issue. She was broken and wounded. When I looked at her, I saw some of myself. Many times I got sick when I left the hospital. I could feel the attacks from fighting for her deliverance. Nevertheless, I persisted. I kept going to sit by her beside. I sang to her, read her scriptures, and encouraged her soul. After several weeks in the hospital, she was finally released. The end of my year was turning out much differently than it began. God was on a roll!

10. IT'S A NEW YEAR

ARE YOU READY FOR THE THINGS YOU'RE PRAYING FOR?

The New Year began with a bang. One afternoon, I was sitting at home reading when my phone rang. It was a lady from my hometown. She wanted to tell me something she had just heard. She asked me if I had spoken to my ex-husband. I had not spoken to him since the divorce. Her next statement shook me to my core. "He's engaged. Your ex-husband is engaged." Wait! What? Was I being punked? How could my ex-husband be engaged? We had only been divorced three months. Although I had no hopes for reconciliation, the news was still very disturbing.

The next obvious question for me was, "Who?" I was almost afraid to ask, but I did. I wasn't really prepared for the response. My ex-husband was engaged to our church photographer. She had photographed us for both of our church anniversary celebrations. My mind immediately started racing, trying to recall dates, times, phone numbers. How long had this been going on?

Immediately my mind went to our first church anniversary as a couple. I had asked him questions about the photographer choice because her demeanor seemed off, and I couldn't quite place it. He had dismissed me as being cantankerous.

The "informant" said the wedding was scheduled for February. I was in shock. He was a pastor. We had only been divorced three months! What was he thinking? Had they already been dating? I rehearsed these thoughts over in my mind. Just as I was poised to move forward with my life, this new revelation came.

Over the next few weeks, random people from my hometown called to "chat" with me. I knew the real reason for their calls. They were fishing for a reaction about my ex-husband. They wanted to see if they could rope me into bashing him. I didn't fall for their antics. I took the high road. I needed to focus on what God was doing with my life. Fixating my attention on his life would be a distraction, one I did not need.

At the beginning of March, I attended a friend's birthday party. We had been friends for 20 years. Toward the end of the party, she told me that she was planning several theme parties for her sister's birthday. One of the parties would be held in Punta Cana. She said I should consider going. It would be fun. The following Monday, she called and told me that God said she should pay for my trip! I was floored. No one had ever done anything like that for me before. A girl's trip was just what I needed to rest and restore, especially in light of the last month's drama.

I booked my flight, and two weeks later, I was boarding a plane. We traveled to the Dominican Republic. Fifteen professional women hit the island for fun in the sun. The beginning of my year was taking shape just like God said. We had a blast. I almost wanted to pinch myself to make sure the trip was real because the experience was so diametrically opposed from my life the previous year.

When I returned, I was scheduled to participate at Career Day for my friend's elementary school. I have to admit I was actually excited. I missed being in schools, teaching and interacting with students. I looked forward to sharing information about my career and spending time with the kindergarteners. They were so precious. They asked lots of questions and seemed genuinely interested in what I had to say. One student had a parent who was a lawyer, but most of them had never heard of a lawyer or an attorney. They were full of energy and life. I left feeling very inspired.

Later in the month, I attended a book writing workshop. One of the ladies at my table began asking me questions about my book and helping me flush out ideas and timelines. She was such a tremendous asset in helping me get back on track. I hadn't done much with my writing, even though I knew I should. I had actually left the book idea in the wind. I hadn't written a thing! I also met an author who had written a book on life after a lay-off. While I hadn't been laid off, I was preparing to launch a brand new career after a five year hiatus. I thought her knowledge and expertise would be useful, so I obtained her information.

I also had been visiting a church near my house fairly regularly. The pastor was very supportive of me and made weekly checks on my progress after the divorce. That meant a lot to me. He was one of the few people who actually showed compassion toward what I endured. He seemed genuinely concerned about my ability to move forward.

The pastor also has a huge heart for missions. The church had begun a partnership in Burkina Faso, so I sponsored a child through their Christmas campaign. A few months later, the church began planning a mission trip there. Every week, I kept feeling a tickle in my heart when I watched the mission video project. It had long been my dream to share the gospel in Africa. I wanted to go. I decided to attend the planning meeting and begin contacting potential sponsors.

One Sunday after church, the pastor's wife approached me. She invited me to speak at a women's event at church. She gave me the date, and I began to prepare. It was exhilarating to prepare for what I was born to do. Almost immediately I knew that I should teach on the woman at the well.

On the day of the event, I got up extra early. I really wanted someone to record the teaching, but I had no one to do it. During my divorce, I was forced to accept a very hard truth. I really didn't have any friends. Most of the people in my life benefitted more from me than I ever had from them. Though I considered myself to be an excellent friend, people had not been the same for me.

I reconciled the fact that I would not have a recording. That would have to come next time. When I arrived, there were about 25 ladies there enjoying brunch. When we transitioned to the teaching portion of the brunch, most of the ladies started giving excuses about why they had to leave. In fact, only five or six ladies stayed. It hurt my feelings that people started leaving, but Holy Spirit didn't allow me to wallow in my disappointment. He reminded me that He was the one who created the opportunity. Even if only one woman was there, her life should be important enough to receive the message He sent! After that rebuke, I was ready to teach without worrying about who stayed or left. The Holy Spirit really is the Master Teacher.

Moving in with my brother landed me in Cumming, Georgia, a suburb outside Atlanta. Some people don't know the city when I say it, but as soon as I mention its county, people take note. Most people, particularly in the South, are well acquainted with Forsyth County. In 1912, the black residents of Forsyth County, a community of 1000, were forced out of the county. They were warned to be gone by sundown or face death. Those 1000 residents were made to leave everything they owned. Property was seized by their white neighbors and considered abandoned. In 1987, Forsyth County received nationwide attention when Oprah Winfrey visited the county. The county's residents were fuming over a civil rights protest held there. They had become very hostile and aggressive. At that time, no black person had lived in Forsyth County for over 75 years. The nation watched as residents talked about "keeping Forsyth white." I share that historical backdrop because when I moved there, I was confronted by racism on more than one occasion.

Once I tried to use a coupon at a local car shop. They refused to take my coupon. When I complained, the owner sent me a threatening letter accusing me of theft. Though I had paid my entire invoice prior to leaving, he wanted to send a message. If I didn't accept their refusal to honor my coupon, I would be arrested and charged with theft of services. He said I actually owed more money than they listed on the invoice. When I opened the letter, I was in shock. I had paid my entire invoice. I was a new lawyer! His false accusations could cause problems for my new career. I ended up having to retain another lawyer to handle the issue. It was handled with one stern letter, but the point still remains that it occurred . . . in 2017!

When I applied for the local bar here, no one responded to my application. I contacted the State Bar and mentioned it to a few people I met at events. Some of the white people I talked to asked me why I didn't just go work for a "black firm in Atlanta." I finally met one white lawyer who agreed to go to lunch with me. When I discussed my experiences, all he could say was how he wished things were different. We had a nice lunch, but he was able to offer me no leads for a job here.

I was finally accepted in the Forsyth bar. It is strange typing that statement because admittance isn't supposed to be optional. If you are a licensed attorney in the state, you apply and you are supposed to be accepted. "Supposed to be" are the operative words there. When I attended my first meeting, I felt like I was on the scene of a film from the 1950s. No one would let me sit at their table. Each empty chair I approached was refused. The lawyers sitting there keep saying the chair belonged to someone else. Finally, I went to the middle of the room and just stood there. I had RSVP'd. Surely one of those seats had to belong to me. No one offered their seat nor did they offer to help me find one. Finally, I went to the back of the room, found a chair by the buffet, and dragged it to the front. Right past all the people in the room. When I stood to introduce myself, I noted that I was a graduate of the University Of Georgia School Of Law. It is likely that somewhere close to 80% of the lawyers in the room were fellow alumni. Afterwards, I thought they would introduce themselves and try to welcome me as the "new kid on the block." That can usually be expected from fellow alumni. I might have been new, but there was no welcome.

The situation was disappointing, but I was determined not to give up. I share these parts of my story to reaffirm the fact that sometimes things happen to you that shouldn't. Sometimes we are treated unfairly and simply get a raw deal. Still, if we persevere and refuse to quit, God can bring great redemption out of something negative.

Besides, by this time I knew too much about God not to trust Him. The things I had endured almost broke me, but they had not, I was still standing. Obviously, God had a plan. I simply needed to trust Him to execute it. Furthermore, my heart was being reawakened to ministry and reaching people for Christ. I was way more passionate about that than being a traditional lawyer anyway.

A couple of weeks later, I went in to talk to the pastor about the mission trip. He asked me if I would be willing to preach on a Sunday in June. I didn't hesitate before saying, "Yes, sure I will!" We talked about a date, and I drove home.

I was really excited. While there were some closed doors in my life, God was opening other ones. He was orchestrating a way for me to share His Word. I counted it as both a privilege and an honor. I immediately began seeking Him for a topic. I knew this particular church needed more instruction on the Holy Spirit, but I didn't want to take the lead. I wanted to deliver whatever word God desired me to give.

Over the course of the next two weeks, I spent time with God, listening to His voice. Finally, he gave me the sermon, "Ten Disciplines of the Believer." It was packed with scripture and practical application. Much of what he gave me would be controversial; it was not at all what most pastors teach. The emphasis was on the Christian's responsibility to follow Jesus' example, change the world, and evangelize the lost. I spent the entire weekend praying and on Sunday, I knew Holy Spirit was with me.

I arrived at church and the pastor greeted me. He was smiling, but he looked a little nervous, "Are you ready?" I looked at him confidently and said, "Yes, Sir, I am!" I had one question for him. "You're not going to talk a lot before I come up are you?" He chuckled. I was anxious to deliver what God had given me, so I didn't want to wait.

Worship was amazing. The worship team was powerful. I sang and lifted my hands. I knew this was my element. Teaching is what I was created to do. The pastor came up and said a little introduction about me. I had been attending the church for over a year. Most of the people already knew me. He called me to the podium, so I came up to the pulpit. I invited the congregation to join me in my favorite song, "How Great Thou Art." I wasn't nervous or anxious like I thought I might be. It was time. God was announcing me. I was far different from the wounded victim that came to this church the year before. God was confirming his stamp of approval.

As I moved through my notes, I left the podium and engaged with the people. Holy Spirit was moving. I could see that they were getting it. I closed the sermon and invited the musicians to the stage. Now it was time for the most important part—the response.

When the Word of God is released, there should always be a response. Praise, worship, repentance, salvation, or demonstration should always follow. I strongly sensed that Holy Spirit was calling for a time of repentance. Of the list He had given, I knew there were some things we were not doing. I invited people to come to the altar and some did. It was a powerful moment. As I ministered to the people, God was completing His work in me. He was making me whole.

After church, the pastor came up to me and said, "You did so good. I'm so proud of you!" I wanted to cry. He was proud of me! I reminisced about all the pain and trauma I had experienced over the past few years. I thought about my parents and grandparents. I reflected on the incredible heritage of faith they instilled in my life. I longed for them to see me. I wanted them to hear me preach. I wanted them to know that I didn't stay broken. I was fighting my way back. After ten years of pain and heartbreak, I was finally moving forward. I wanted them to know.

11.   SENSITIVITY TRAINING

CAN GOD TRUST YOU TO LISTEN
TO HIS VOICE?

Anticipation was building for the mission trip. I raised more than enough money from my sponsors, so I started preparing for the trip. I had never been to Africa, and I had never done missions. I had learned a lot about spiritual warfare, and I knew it would be fierce. Whenever you seek to advance the Gospel, there is always opposition. I wanted to build cohesiveness with the team and develop a prayer strategy. Most of the team members already knew each other, but I did not know them well.

I had lots of questions. I am very detailed, so I wanted to walk through every facet of the trip. The more I asked questions, the more uncomfortable I felt. There were too many details that were still unresolved. The more I asked questions, the more agitated the team seemed to become. I started to feel very uneasy.

The week before we were scheduled to leave, I asked about registering with the Embassy. I would never have considered the need if it had not been for one of my friends. She travels back and forth to Africa all the time. When I registered, I discovered that Burkina Faso was under a travel warning. The description of the warning gave me pause. The verbiage of the warning basically indicated that anyone who ignored the warning would do so at their own peril. The United States had no intention of providing any assistance to evacuate in the case of an emergency. The warning also referenced a terrorist attack the previous year that specifically targeted tourists. Each line I read caused me to take a deeper breath. I knew God would protect me. I didn't want to be fearful, but I wanted to use wisdom. Besides, the mission was less than a week away.

That Saturday evening, I discussed my plight with my family. I told my nephew to read the warning. When he got to the country name, his girlfriend screamed, "Where?" My nephew repeated himself, "Burkina Faso!" His girlfriend stammered, "My friend was there last year during that attack!" I couldn't believe what I was hearing. She actually knew a survivor of the attack. I had to talk to her. My nephew's girlfriend texted me an article about her friend and gave me her phone number. We scheduled a time to talk the next day. By this time, I was leaning heavily toward dropping from the team. I didn't have peace about the trip.

I went to church Sunday morning with a very heavy heart. God had promised to send me to the nations. I had a heart for Africa. All the money had been raised. I even had gotten the six immunization shots I needed. Ouch! How could this be happening? Everything had seemed so perfect.

I cried. I prayed. I prayed. I cried. I could not hear anything from God. I walked into church almost in tears. How would I tell the pastor? How would I tell the team? Our flight was scheduled in less than seven days. The timing was all wrong. Really wrong. The pastor preached a sermon about missions, and there were large packed suitcases lined across the front of the church.

When he completed his sermon, he called the team forward for prayer—one by one. My heart was thumping in my chest. Should I go forward? Should I remain in my seat? I hadn't gotten the chance to talk to the pastor before service. He didn't know I had changed my mind about going. I had to think fast. He was calling my name. I decided to go forward. I would not cause a scene. I walked from my seat and joined the line. As soon as I joined the line, I felt like I had a frog in my throat. My eyes started watering. What was my face doing? The entire church was looking at me. Just as I tried to think of something else, they started. My emotions were betraying me. Ripples of tears began flowing down my face. My only saving grace was that my body didn't start doing the accompanying cry jerk! I was a mess.

The pastor called someone to come pray for us and he made his way down the line. Why did he start at the other end? I needed to sit down. I tried not to make eye contact with anyone in the audience. It seemed like hours passed before he got to me. When the member laid hands on me, he began to prophesy. He said God was going to use me mightily. I had been called to missions and God's power would follow me there. This would only be the beginning of what God planned to do in my life. Wow! Just when I thought my tear ducts were depleted, they started again. I needed him to hurry up. The emotion was embarrassing.

When church was over, I tried to hurry out. The member who had prayed caught me. Dang! I tried to give a fake smile as he came close. "Are you okay? You look like something is bothering you." I said, "I'm okay." He didn't look convinced, but I didn't give him time for further interrogation. I slid past him, out the door, into my car.

All night I labored over the decision. My heart longed to reach Africa. I wanted to take the Gospel there. This was my destiny. That Sunday was really tough. About 10:00, I finally began to have peace about my decision. I wasn't going. I was backing out. I tried to call the pastor; I sent a text to his wife, and I called the church administrator. I didn't want to seem like coward, but since none of them answered their phones, I was forced to leave messages for them.

I was totally perplexed by the turn of events. I had a mandate for Africa. Prophecy had confirmed that. The provision for the trip was easily raised, yet I was not going. It is during times like these that our faith is tested. We are challenged to decide what we really believe about God. It is easy to serve Him when things go as we planned, but when He says," No, Not yet, or Wait" there is a choice to be made. Either we believe He always knows what is best or we pout and complain like spoiled children. My response . . . was somewhere in between the two.

The team left that week, and I decided to contact my sponsors. I needed to be accountable for the money they donated. I reached out to them and shared the travel warning. For most of them that was enough. They fully supported my decision. Most tried to reassure me that there would be other trips. I wasn't so sure. My life had been pretty unpredictable. When else would I have a week to go to Africa? I hoped I'd be working soon.

I tried to reach one of my sponsors, but I got his voicemail. I left him a message, but I also sent him a text. In about ten minute's time, he called me back.

"Ms. Mayfield? How are you?"

"I am very conflicted and disappointed right now. I thought I was going to Africa."

"Well, actually, that's why I'm calling you. I am taking a mission team to Africa, too. I didn't want to say anything earlier because you were going with another team, but now. .

But now, what? What was he going to say? I braced myself for his next line. "Well, I was going to ask you if you'd still like to go to Africa." Was he kidding? Of course I wanted to go to Africa, but how? When?

"Well, our team leaves in one month. We booked our flights yesterday, so you'd have to make a decision pretty quickly. What do you think?"

I asked him for more details about the trip. "Well, we are going to Africa for 10 days and Jerusalem for five." Wait! Did he just say Africa and Jerusalem—in one trip! I wanted to drop the phone and run. Now I understood why I had not been able to go on the original trip. I was going on a trip that combined two of my dreams in one—missions in Africa and a pilgrimage to Jerusalem. Jeremiah 29:1 declares: For I know the thoughts that I think toward you, thoughts of peace, and not of evil, to give you a future and a hope. Our God is full of surprises!

EPILOGUE

Famous Bible teacher, Joyce Meyer, teaches often about God putting us on the shelf for a period of preparation and pruning. God often uses a period of obscurity to hide us until we are ready to walk out His plan. His timing is impeccable. He knows exactly where we are and how to bring his plan to fruition. We must believe Him through the process of becoming. We must learn to trust Him in the dark.

There may be a tremendous call on your life for ministry or to have some level of tremendous influence in one of the mountains of culture. Maybe you are an artist, a CEO, or a very skilled carpenter. Just because you are now working behind the scenes does not change God's plan for your destiny. God uses the time of hiding to perfect our character, teach us who he is, strengthen our faith, and ensure that we have the skills for the assignment. We can overcome obstacles and face down depression and death. As we do, our lives serve as living monuments of the enduring power of God. We become living epistles, read of all men. 2 Corinthians 3:2.

When we encounter difficulty and disappointment, we often forget God's promise to work all things together for our good. We get fixated on the pain and forget that nothing lasts forever. Still, God is always at work, perfecting us and making us more like him. When we submit to the process, we begin to see growth and acceleration in the spiritual realm. We receive promotions which move us closer to being people of great influence. Most importantly, at every juncture, God proves that He can be trusted.

As you experience challenges in your own life, remember to trust God with the process. Look for Him at every juncture. In every second of every moment, know that

He is speaking to you. In great blessing, He is there. Even in tremendous adversity, He can be counted on to sustain you. Endeavor to look for the value in each step of your journey, remembering that God's ultimate goal is to make you like him. The next time something very unexpected or unnatural occurs in your life, stop, look and listen. God will speak to your heart and reveal His next steps for you. The revelation may at first seem overwhelming, but embrace it as God's plan for your life. Your life after the encounter will never be the same.

Everything in my life has prepared me for this moment. A year ago, I faced one of the greatest trials of my life, but today I stand stronger, wiser and I am being used daily by God to reach His people with my story. My encounter with the Burning Bush enabled me to experience another aspect of His infinite character. I know now Him as Provider, Sustainer, and Comforter. Most importantly, I have come to experience Him as Abba, my Daddy God. He has taken a difficult season in my life and used it to grow my character and draw me closer to Him. Better still, I have learned that I am far stronger than I ever thought I was.

It is my prayer that this book has inspired you to overcome obstacles and look for the silver lining in every situation. Some things you endure may not even be about you; they may simply be something you face to strengthen others in their journey. As long as you remain hopeful, nothing is impossible.

God is weaving a tapestry of great wealth and beauty from your life. Your story deserves to be told and celebrated. Though you may have a few battle scars, do not stop! You owe it to the world to be all God created you to be. If ever you feel like you can't make it, remember me, and remember my story. Despite everything that happened, I am still standing, and so are you! Be motivated and encouraged to keep going! With God as your Father, nothing can stop you. The journey of a lifetime awaits you in "Connecting with the Burning Bush!"

MAKING YOUR HEART LIGHTER, LLC

Mission:

There are times when navigating life challenges takes a toll on the heart and a mental health professional is needed. I am willing to walk with you on this journey until your heart feels lighter.

Specialty Areas:

Clinical Supervision, Individual/Group Therapy (mental health, social skills development, substance abuse, anger management, grief/loss, Christian counseling), Training/Staff Development, Suicide Prevention, Consultation, Sports Psychology (Basketball) & mobile counseling

Clinical Services for:

Adults/Young Adults/ Adolescents, Service Members & Family, Offender Populations (Adults/ Juveniles), At-Risk Youths, Mental Health Professionals & Correctional Staff and Athletes

Our Locations:

106 Colony Park Drive Suite 500
Cumming, GA 30040

950 Dannon View Suite 4201
Atlanta, GA 30331

Dr. Angela Powell Smith

Office: 678-771-5920   Fax: 470-253-8191
www.makingyourheartlighter.com

PRIMERICA®

Betty Ann Rucker
Division Leader

If you died today, and I attended your funeral, which of the following do you think your family would find more valueable?

A. $20 donated to GoFundMe
B. A condolence card
C. A dish of food
D. An arrangement of flowers
E. A check that would cover the cost of the funeral, remaining medical bills, pay off all debt owed, provide college money for the children, and replace years of lost income

If the answer is E, message me and let's sit down and talk.

Phone Number : 706-436-4216
Email : bettyannrucker@gmail.com

An independent representative of Primerica

55886145R00095

Made in the USA
Columbia, SC
22 April 2019